SAGE was founded in 1965 by Sara Miller McCune to support the dissemination of usable knowledge by publishing innovative and high-quality research and teaching content. Today, we publish more than 750 journals, including those of more than 300 learned societies, more than 800 new books per year, and a growing range of library products including archives, data, case studies, reports, conference highlights, and video. SAGE remains majority-owned by our founder, and after Sara's lifetime will become owned by a charitable trust that secures our continued independence.

Los Angeles | London | Washington DC | New Delhi | Singapore | Boston

Globalization of Legal Services and Regulatory Reforms

Globalization of Legal Services and Regulatory Reforms

Perspectives and Dynamics from India

Rupa Chanda
Pralok Gupta

www.sagepublications.com
Los Angeles • London • New Delhi • Singapore • Washington DC • Boston

Copyright © Rupa Chanda and Pralok Gupta, 2015

All rights reserved. No part of this book may be reproduced or utilized in any form or by any means, electronic or mechanical, including photocopying, recording or by any information storage or retrieval system, without permission in writing from the publisher.

First published in 2015 by

SAGE Publications India Pvt Ltd
B1/I-1 Mohan Cooperative Industrial Area
Mathura Road, New Delhi 110 044, India
www.sagepub.in

SAGE Publications Inc
2455 Teller Road
Thousand Oaks, California 91320, USA

SAGE Publications Ltd
1 Oliver's Yard, 55 City Road
London EC1Y 1SP, United Kingdom

SAGE Publications Asia-Pacific Pte Ltd
3 Church Street
#10-04 Samsung Hub
Singapore 049483

Published by Vivek Mehra for SAGE Publications India Pvt Ltd, typeset at 11/13.5 pts Bembo by Diligent Typesetter, Delhi and printed at Sai Print-o-Pack New Delhi.

Library of Congress Cataloging-in-Publication Data

Chanda, Rupa, author.
  Globalization of legal services and regulatory reforms : perspectives and dynamics from India / Rupa Chanda and Pralok Gupta.
     pages cm
  Includes bibliographical references and index.
  1. Legal services—India. I. Gupta, Pralok, author. II. Title.
  KNS53.3C48   347.54—dc23   2015   2015004824

ISBN: 978-93-515-0143-5 (HB)

The SAGE Team: N. Unni Nair, Neha Sharma, Nand Kumar Jha and Vinitha Nair

Dedicated to our parents

Smt. Kabita Chanda
and
Sh. Ramesh Chanda
Rupa Chanda

Late Smt. Krishna Devi
and
Late Sh. Surya Prakash Gupta
Pralok Gupta

Thank you for choosing a SAGE product! If you have any comment, observation or feedback, I would like to personally hear from you. Please write to me at contactceo@sagepub.in

—Vivek Mehra, Managing Director and CEO,
SAGE Publications India Pvt Ltd, New Delhi

Bulk Sales

SAGE India offers special discounts for purchase of books in bulk. We also make available special imprints and excerpts from our books on demand.

For orders and enquiries, write to us at

Marketing Department
SAGE Publications India Pvt Ltd
B1/I-1, Mohan Cooperative Industrial Area
Mathura Road, Post Bag 7
New Delhi 110044, India
E-mail us at marketing@sagepub.in

Get to know more about SAGE, be invited to SAGE events, get on our mailing list. Write today to marketing@sagepub.in

This book is also available as an e-book.

Contents

List of Tables	ix
List of Figures	xi
List of Abbreviations	xiii
Preface	xv
Acknowledgments	xix
1 Globalization and Regulation of Professional Services	1
2 Trade in Legal Services: Past and Present Trends	17
3 Regulatory Environment for Legal Services: A Cross-country Analysis	38
4 Legal Services in India	69
5 Political Economy of Liberalization: Stakeholders' Views	93
6 A Roadmap for Reforms	155
Annexure	165
Bibliography	192
Index	199
About the Authors	203

List of Tables

2.1	Top Ranked 20 Law Firms	29
2.2	World Bank Overall and Modal Restrictiveness Indices for Legal Services, 2010	36
3.1	OECD Indicators for Legal Services, Selected Years	67
3.2	OECD Indicators for Entry and Conduct Regulations for Legal Services, Selected Years	68
4.1	India's Legal Services Exports and Imports (in US$ Millions), 2004–2010	85
A.1	OECD Services Trade Restrictiveness Index (STRI) Regulations for Legal Services	165
A.2	World Bank Modal Restrictions in Legal Services for Selected Countries	168
A.3	Entry and Conduct Regulations Used for Calculating OECD Indicator	179
A.4	Legal Services Commitments by Korea in India–Korea CEPA	182
A.5	Legal Services Commitments by Japan in India–Japan CEPA	184
A.6	Legal Services Commitments by Singapore in India–Singapore CECA	191

List of Figures

2.1 The Legal Services Market in the US, Europe, Asia-Pacific, and the World, 2013   26

2.2 Global Legal Services Market Segmentation, 2013 and 2010   27

2.3 Percentage Growth of Top 50 Legal Firms, 1998/99–2007/08   29

2.4 OECD Services Trade Restrictiveness Index (STRI) for Legal Services, 2014   34

2.5 World Bank Overall and Modal Restrictiveness Indices for Legal Services, 2010   37

3.1 Trends in OECD Indicators for Legal Services for Selected Countries   66

4.1 India's Legal Services Exports and Imports (in US$ Millions), 2004–2010   85

List of Abbreviations

ABA	American Bar Association
ABSs	Alternative Business Structures
AUD	Australian Dollar
AIBE	All India Bar Examination
BCI	Bar Council of India
BPO	Business Process Outsourcing
BPTC	Bar Professional Training Course
CA	Chartered Accountants
CAGR	Compound Annual Growth Rate
CLE	Continuing Legal Education
CPC	Central Product Classification
CPD	Continuing Professional Development
EC	European Community
EU	European Union
FDI	Foreign Direct Investment
FIPB	Foreign Investment Promotion Board
FLA	Formal Law Alliance
FLC	Foreign Legal Consultant
FLFs	Foreign Law Firms
FTA	Free Trade Agreements
GATS	General Agreement on Trade in Services
GATT	General Agreement on Tariffs and Trade
GJB	Gaikokuho-Jimu-Bengoshi
IPO	Initial Public Offering
IPR	Intellectual Property Rights
JD	Juris Doctor
JETCO	Joint Economic and Trade Committee

JFBA	Japanese Federation of Bar Associations
JLV	Joint Law Venture
JV	Joint Ventures
LLB	Bachelor of Laws
LLP	Limited Liability Partnership
LPA	Legal Profession Act
LPC	Legal Practice Course
LPO	Legal Process Outsourcing
MDPs	Multidisciplinary Partnerships
MNC	Multinational Corporations
MRA	Mutual Recognition Agreements
NAFTA	North American Free Trade Agreement
NSW	New South Wales
OECD	Organization for Economic Co-operation and Development
PLC	Postgraduate Law Course
PLT	Practical Legal Training
PPP	Public–Private Partnership
PRC	People's Republic of China
PSC	Professional Skills Course
PTAs	Preferential Trade Agreements
PTO	Pupillage Training Organization
QFLF	Qualified Foreign Law Firm
RBI	Reserve Bank of India
REL	Registered European Lawyer
RTA	Regional Trade Agreement
SMEs	Small and Medium Enterprises
SRA	Solicitors Regulation Authority
STRI	Services Trade Restrictiveness Index
TISA	Trade in Services Agreement
UK	United Kingdom
UN	United Nations
UNCPC	United Nations Central Product Classification
US	United States of America
WTO	World Trade Organization

Preface*

The domestic regulatory environment in India's legal services sector is currently restrictive; though, in recent years, there have been tentative steps toward making this sector globally more competitive. However, the focus has remained on introducing piecemeal changes rather than addressing the inherent and structural deficiencies in this sector or in preparing it for the long-term needs of the economy. There is a growing external pressure on India to open up its legal services sector and to provide market access to foreign firms. At the same time, there are also growing internal pressures and compulsions to not allow access to foreign firms. The problematic issue is that domestic regulatory reforms that are needed to strengthen this sector and to build its capacity tend to get equated with the subject of liberalizing legal services. As a consequence, it is often forgotten that the primary issue facing this sector is not that of liberalization and providing access to foreign firms but rather the need to address the weaknesses and

---

*Disclaimer: This book has been produced for research and academic purposes only. While all care has been taken to provide correct information, the authors do not assure correctness of information taken from secondary sources, as mentioned in the book. The authors assume no responsibility for any injury or damage of whatsoever nature to any person or organization from using the information provided in this book.

The views and opinions contained in this book are of those who participated in the survey and consultations organized in the course of the study. The book attempts to understand the different sides of the arguments and views expressed and to analyze the basis for these opinions and their implications for the sector. The discussion presented in the book does not reflect any endorsement or position taken by the authors on the subject.

regulatory gaps that affect its global competitiveness and its ability to serve the emerging needs of the Indian economy. Thus, the need of the hour is to prepare this sector for greater competition in future and for the changing economic realities in India and globally. There is an urgent need to create a roadmap for regulatory reforms and for strengthening capacity in India's legal services sector.

Against this backdrop, this book attempts to understand the prevailing dynamics in this sector in India. It analyzes the perspectives of a representative set of stakeholders regarding the various regulatory and structural shortcomings in India's legal services sector and also regarding the opening up of this sector. It examines the validity of these perspectives, the factors underlying the expressed views and concerns and tries to arrive at a balanced assessment of the issues surrounding reforms and liberalization in India's legal services. It also attempts to provide policy inputs and suggestions for strengthening the regulatory framework and capacity in this sector and provides the basic contours which such strengthening would involve, by focusing on specific regulatory amendments as well as forward looking measures such as harmonization with international standards, adoption of best practices from other countries, investment in education and training, and possible reorganization of existing regulatory structures and mandates.

The book is based on a project titled "Strengthening Regulatory Frameworks and Enhancing Capacity in India's Legal and Accountancy Services Sectors: A Roadmap for Reforms", carried out by the authors between November 2011 and May 2013. The project was funded by the Foreign and Commonwealth Office, New Delhi, under its India Prosperity Fund.

The findings and analysis presented in this book are based on secondary research as well as discussions with relevant stakeholders. The secondary research focused on the available literature on services sector reforms and liberalization issues, the prevailing regulatory environment in India's legal services, the experience of other countries with regard to capacity building and reforms in this sector, and an examination of regulatory practices and frameworks across selected developed and developing countries. The primary research comprised of round tables with stakeholders representing various segments within the legal services sector, as well as in-depth discussions carried out with practitioners and academics in person and over the telephone.

Rupa Chanda
Pralok Gupta

Acknowledgments

We are thankful to all the respondents who took part in the primary survey work of this study, and who provided us with useful insights and suggestions to help us understand the regulatory environment in the legal services sector. We also express our gratitude toward all the stakeholders who attended the consultation meetings organized during the study both in India and in the United Kingdom (UK) as well as the organizers of these meetings in both the countries. A special note of gratitude is due to Kirthiga Balasubramaniam, research assistant at the Indian Institute of Management, Bangalore, for providing timely and competent research and administrative support throughout the study. We also sincerely thank our parent institutions, Indian Institute of Management, Bangalore, and Centre for WTO Studies, Indian Institute of Foreign Trade, New Delhi, for providing a congenial environment to work on this manuscript. Last but not the least, we thank the Foreign and Commonwealth Office and its staff in India for extending financial and administrative support and for making this study possible.

1
Globalization and Regulation of Professional Services

The globalization of professional services and its consequent implications for their regulation has been a subject of considerable debate and reflection since the 1990s. Watershed developments such as the North American Free Trade Agreement (NAFTA) signed in 1992 and the World Trade Organization's (WTO) General Agreement on Trade in Services (GATS) signed in 1994, both of which widened the ambit of trade discussions to cover services including professional services, were probably the first to draw attention to this issue in a focused manner. The subject has gained further traction through the past two decades given the visible growth in international trade and investment flows in professional services. Cross-border establishment of firms, cross-border movement of professionals, outsourcing arrangements, and the advent of information and communication technologies have enabled the globalization of a wide range of professions such as accounting, legal, architecture, engineering, and management consulting services.

Although the definition of a business or professional service and what is meant by the globalization of such services remain a matter of debate, a point that is well recognized in the extant literature on professional services is their many distinctive characteristics. The high degree of customization, the reliance on domain knowledge and expertise, intangible assets and networks as a source of competitiveness, the presence of incumbency advantages, the importance of size and scope in shaping market power, special organizational and operational formats, and market failures in the form of information asymmetry make professional services distinctive in many ways from other activities. However, these very characteristics in turn pose unique challenges and complexities in regulating professional services, especially in the wake of their liberalization and growing global competition. While regulation of professional service markets has typically been justified on the grounds of market failure which needs to be addressed in public interest, increasingly, regulators around the world, and especially in developing countries, are facing difficulties in designing regulations that can adapt to changing market realities. These difficulties are arising due to the competitive challenges posed by foreign providers, paradigm shifts in how professional services are perceived, and technological developments.

Thus far, the discussion on globalization of professional services in the context of multilateral, regional, and bilateral negotiations and in the extant literature has been marked by debate on two interlinked dimensions. The first dimension of the debate concerns the regulation of professional services in the wake of globalization, i.e., the extent to which these services should be regulated and how to most effectively regulate them so as to benefit from as well as confront the challenges posed by globalization. Key to this line of debate have been issues of recognition, standards, licensing and qualification procedures, restrictions pertaining to fees, advertising and other operating conditions and various "behind-the-border" barriers. The debate concerns the extent to which these regulations may be warranted, and whether they may be unduly burdensome and might stifle competition. Although this challenge of balancing the need for pro-competitive regulation is not unique to professional services, the factors which distinguish professional services from other activities are their highly specialized and customized nature and their often jurisdiction-specific standards and requirements, which may justify differential regulatory approaches across countries. This adds a layer of complexity to the usual debate over what constitutes adequate and necessary regulation when we discuss professional services. Moreover, with globalization, an additional issue that arises is whether and how to realign existing regulations and regulatory structures and institutions.

The second dimension of the debate concerns the impact of professional services liberalization in terms of its implications for the cost of these services, their quality, standards, variety, market structure and segmentation, employment, and the possibilities for economies of scale and scope. Once again, while some of these concerns are not unique to professional services, a concern specific to these services stems from the significance of professional codes of conduct, ethics, and practice, and the presence of information failure in such markets. This relates to concerns over the possible violation of existing codes of conduct and eluding of regulators following liberalization, with adverse consequences for the domestic market. The latter in turn brings to the fore the question of regulatory and institutional preparedness and capacity to cope with liberalization and its effects.

Thus, as the various aspects of the debate highlight, the core issue surrounding the liberalization and regulation of professional services is the need to protect professional interests without sacrificing the larger public interest, to ensure regulatory autonomy without sacrificing competitiveness, and to identify an appropriate regulatory framework, especially when confronted with globalization pressures in order to balance these potentially conflicting objectives. It is therefore not surprising that with the globalization of professional services, many countries have had to revisit their regulatory approach to these services and have been forced to reregulate them.

It is important to recognize, however, that although professional services regulation and liberalization is governed by certain common principles and organizational formats, there is also considerable heterogeneity across professions. Hence, the significance of the aforementioned issues and debates varies across different professional services. While some professions such as management consulting or information technology do not require accreditation, others such as medical, architectural, accounting, and legal services are licensed professions. The regulatory concerns regarding standards, assurance of quality, and procedural requirements in such accredited services are necessarily much greater. But even among the accredited professions, there are differences, and the degree of sensitivity on issues of liberalization and regulatory reforms varies. While professions such as accounting and auditing services, though accredited nationally, are subject to certain international standards and practices and are more comparable across countries in terms of the content and systems of training, others such as legal services are highly bound by jurisdictional requirements and systems of practice, which makes them inherently more prone to regulatory challenges and sensitivities when confronted with the forces of internationalization.

Outline and Objectives

This book focuses on one particular professional service, legal services. The choice of this sector is in part motivated by the strident nature of the debate on regulation and liberalization in the legal services sector given some of its specific characteristics. There is thus a need to assess the extent to which the nature of the discussion in this sector resonates with that found in other professional services and where this sector may differ.

This book highlights the regulatory challenges and perceptions surrounding legal services liberalization in a developing economy such as India, where many professional services remain subject to regulatory restrictions and where the debate over regulation of professional services is at an interesting juncture, caught between the proponents and opponents of liberalization and reforms. The discussion draws upon both secondary and primary evidences and is guided by two broad objectives. The first objective is to assess the relevance of arguments commonly presented in the literature on professional services liberalization and regulation in the context of a specific emerging market such as India and for a specific sector such as legal services and additionally to also identify sector and market-specific issues and concerns. The second objective is to derive insights from the secondary and primary evidence on possible approaches to reforming the regulatory setup and measures affecting the legal services in a restrictive market such as India, so as to strengthen the sector to face the challenges posed by globalization and to help prepare it for eventual liberalization in the future. Hence, the focus is not on liberalization per se, but on how to build capacity and evolve regulations and the regulatory setup given changing market realities.

The discussion that follows in the rest of this chapter provides an overview of the literature on regulating professional services and the rationale commonly advanced in these studies for various regulatory measures that are commonly applied in these services. The aim of this chapter is to provide the broad analytical framework within which the subsequent discussion specific to legal services is to be placed. The idea is to provide an introduction to the basic principles, particular features, conceptual issues, debates, and regulatory and institutional approaches that characterize professional services and thus to provide the context for understanding and analyzing the case of legal services in India, which is the focus of this book.

Chapter 2 next turns to the legal services sector and its globalization, highlighting global trends in the sector with regard to the internationalization of legal practice through trade, investment, and mobility. It discusses landmark developments such as the GATS and NAFTA as well as other notable developments in the regulatory evolution of the legal services sector in leading provider markets such as the US (United States of America) and the UK (United Kingdom). This chapter also presents various regulatory indices that have been developed by multilateral organizations such as the World Bank and the Organization for Economic Co-operation and Development (OECD) to measure the incidence of regulatory measures in this sector across key developed and emerging economies. This is followed by Chapter 3 which provides a relatively detailed account of key regulations that prevail in this sector across a selected set of countries to highlight the variation in regulatory approach across countries and the kinds of issues that are important in understanding the discourse on liberalization and deregulation of legal services.

Chapter 4 next discusses the specifics of the legal services sector and its regulation in India. It highlights particular statutes and legislations that are pertinent to the regulation of this sector. It discusses India's foreign direct investment (FDI) policy in legal services and its domestic regulations concerning scale, scope, organizational formats, fees, advertising, and other such areas where professional services tend to be face restrictions. The chapter also presents India's stance on the liberalization of legal services under the GATS and under its many comprehensive economic integration agreements and highlights the lack of proactive engagement by India on issues such as mutual recognition and mobility of legal professionals. The discussion in this chapter aims to illustrate the country's rather defensive policy orientation in legal services, and its reluctance to make binding commitments in this sector under international agreements.

Chapter 5 next presents the findings of a small-scale survey that was carried out to elicit the views and perceptions of a range of stakeholders on legal services liberalization and regulatory reforms and priorities in the Indian context. This survey, which was administered to small and large Indian firms, international firms, law associations, regulators, and sector experts, through in-person, telephonic, and remote means, threw up a mix of views regarding the need to regulate legal services and what form such regulation must take. The discussion in this chapter highlights these mixed views and in particular the points made by respondents in support of and in opposition to the liberalization of legal services. It also examines the validity of these arguments in light of the literature on professional services.

Chapter 6 summarizes the main insights that emerge from the analysis in earlier chapters and outlines a possible roadmap for initiating regulatory reforms in India's legal services sector.

The discussion draws upon the extant literature on regulation in professional services as well as the experiences of other countries which have undergone a regulatory transformation and opening up of their legal services sectors. The chapter concludes by highlighting the importance of developing capacity and strengthening the legal services sector in a growing economy like India where there is growing presence of foreign businesses and also growing interest on the part of Indian businesses to go global. As this chapter argues, managing legal services regulation in the context of a globalizing economy is critical given the supporting role of legal services in facilitating domestic and foreign businesses and thus in enabling integration with world markets.

The following sections of this chapter address the key conceptual and analytical issues that are at the heart of any discussion on the globalization of professional services and which are needed to better understand the arguments for and against regulatory reforms and liberalization of a sector such as legal services. The following discussion highlights the rationale for regulating professional services, the modalities for such regulation, and the implications of liberalizing professional services.

Regulating Professional Services

It is widely accepted in the economic literature that professional services need to be regulated as free markets for professional services do not lead to efficient outcomes. This is due to the presence of market failures (Van den Bergh 2006; Dingwall and Fenn 1987). The most important form of market failure in professional services is asymmetric information, i.e., consumers are not able to discern the capability of the service provider as they need a high level of technical knowledge and domain expertise to evaluate them. This gives rise to the standard problems of adverse selection and moral hazard in such markets. The second problem concerns the negative externalities that may arise to third parties and society from bad performance of contracts between providers and consumers of professional services. The third market failure pertains to the public good nature of these services and the positive externalities that may arise from the provision of professional services. To address all these market failures, regulation of quality is a necessary response to protect consumer interests, to assure minimum standards and quality and to internalize the externalities.

However, while the academic literature accepts the need to regulate professional services, there is a considerable debate about what form this regulation should take. The issue here is whether information remedies are sufficient or whether there is a need to directly regulate quality. It has been argued that a proportionality principle should be applied, i.e., regulations should be in proportion to the desired objective, which means they should be deemed necessary and adequate and not unduly burdensome. This is a principle that has also been accepted by the Working Party on Domestic Regulation under the GATS. The economics of regulation suggests the need to take a cost-benefit approach to the matter. A regulation should be introduced only if its benefits exceed its costs and thus to use direct quality control through regulation only when information remedies are not sufficient to correct the information asymmetry problem. The difficulty here is how to assess what constitutes adequate regulation that is proportional to a given objective. Further, who should decide this?

This brings one to another important question that always plagues the regulation of professional services, i.e., who should regulate the professions, the state or the profession itself. The core debate here concerns the pros and cons of self-regulation.[1] The latter implies that the professionalized occupation has strong control over the practice of the profession as the nodal association certifies membership, based on demonstrated expertise and adherence to certain codes of conduct. This in effect implies a self-regulated monopoly. The literature on self-regulation points out both benefits and costs of this regulatory approach. There are benefits in the form of greater flexibility, internalization of regulatory costs within the

---

[1] See Van den Bergh (2006) for further discussion on self-regulation in professions.

profession and the advantage of domain knowledge and expertise that an insider to the profession possesses over the state. However, self-regulation can result in the abuse of regulatory powers to thwart competition due to disproportionate regulation. It can result in high-entry barriers to ensure high profits for the members of the profession, lack of accountability to outsiders, rent-seeking behavior, and regulatory capture. In particular, control over certification by the profession creates the scope for introducing entry barriers into the occupation. Self-regulation also tends to limit competition within the profession and may contribute to asymmetric information. This is because competition among professionals to woo clients is usually discouraged in professional services as it is perceived as hurting quality and causing adverse selection among service providers. So, on grounds of preserving trustworthiness and ensuring quality based on reputation, professional codes usually prohibit various kinds of commercially competitive behavior such as soliciting clients, advertising, and competing on price, although there are differences in quality among professionals and permitting such a competition can help improve quality.

The key concern with self-regulation therefore is the adverse impact it can have on competition, in terms of entry into the profession and within the profession. Evidence from countries and across professions confirms the competition thwarting effects of regulation. Van den Bergh (2006) cites a study of different European Community (EC) member states and professions which found that the higher the intensity of regulation, smaller was the number of professionals and higher were the earnings per professional. Countries with lower degrees of regulation exhibited lower revenues per professional but a larger number of practicing professionals and much higher overall turnover. Hence, evidence seems to suggest a tradeoff between the incidence of regulation and the wider social interest.

From a policy perspective, the main issue confronting policy makers is whether the profession should or should not be allowed to retain monopolistic powers. The answer depends on the overall assessment of the welfare implications of regulation by the state as opposed to regulation by the professional body. But the latter is difficult to determine. For example, do the competition muting effects of self-regulation and the resulting impact on the price, quality, variety, and availability of services outweigh the information signaling that self-regulation makes possible about the quality of the service, which consumers cannot readily measure by themselves? What is the objective function that the profession seeks to optimize? At one extreme, the profession could be seen as maximizing its per capita income and on the other extreme it could be perceived as maximizing some measure of social welfare by regulating the quality of entrants into the sector or something in between which is to maximize producer surplus. How do the welfare of consumers and the income of the professions' members vary with the number of players, the size, market structure and quality of the profession? Is there an inherent conflict between a policy maker's objective to maximize consumer welfare and the self-regulating profession's objective to maximize its members' incomes?[2] There are thus numerous issues which need to be considered to arrive at a judgment on what constitutes an appropriate regulatory setup, who is to regulate and how, and what constitutes necessary and adequate regulation. It is thus not surprising that the literature on the regulation of professions remains ambivalent.

Organization theory highlights some other issues which make the regulation of professional services problematic. These studies note the fact that professionals are autonomous individuals and hence their preferences are inherently in conflict with the hierarchies of commercially oriented organizational structures (Von Nordenflecht 2010). This latter characteristic makes professional partnerships the dominant organizational form for many professional services, especially professions such as accounting and law where reputation and trust-based relationships are very important. Such an organizational form enables the professional to have more bargaining power and makes the organization very dependent on the professional's skills

---

[2] See Shaked and Sutton (1981) for a theoretical exposition of these welfare issues.

and competence. These features of professional services firms in turn further complicate the regulation of professional services because of the autonomous nature of most professional services entities and the partnership format of operation, making it harder for the state to regulate such services.

The debate over regulatory form and content in professional services continues. Both developed and developing economies are confronted with these challenges and several have undergone changes in their regulatory approach and frameworks in the last two decades. Drawing upon the law and economics literature, these approaches involve creating institutional frameworks which enable the realization of the advantages of self-regulation while minimizing its adverse effects. This involves co-regulation via an appropriate division of regulatory powers between the state and professional bodies, and through competitive self-regulation by creating competition between professional bodies and instituting ways to improve the accountability of self-regulatory bodies to the state and the public. Broadly, there is a gradual shift away from pure self-regulation toward greater involvement by the state in many countries.

Liberalizing Professional Services

A related issue that is at the heart of current discussions on professional services is their liberalization, how and to what extent it should be undertaken and what are its resulting effects on the sector and on the wider economy. The discussion is rooted in usual trade theory arguments.[3] Opening up of the economy to international competition involves removing barriers to the flow of goods and services across countries. According to trade theory, this entails adjustment costs on the previously protected sectors. There is potential displacement of domestic providers by competing imports, shifting of resources to other sectors or to other

---

[3] See Majluf and Zarrilli (2007) and Tullao (1999) for discussion on liberalization of professional services.

firms within the sector which are more competitive and relocation and training costs in order to adjust to increased competition. If foreign players have market power, then liberalization may entail additional costs by displacing small local competitors, raising prices, and segmenting the market between small and large players, between domestic and foreign firms. However, trade liberalization can also yield potential benefits in terms of increased efficiency, better allocation of resources, realization of economies of scale and scope, transfer of knowledge and technology, and improvement in standards.

The issues are no different in the context of professional services liberalization. Studies on professional services highlight similar costs and benefits of opening up professional services sectors. Trade liberalization in professional services can potentially facilitate the cross-border mobility of professionals, the importing of skills and expertise, entry into cross-border collaborative arrangements between professionals enhancing mutual learning and sharing of regulatory experience and also professional incomes. Overall, liberalization of professional services can help raise professional standards and provide access to a greater variety and better quality of such services. These benefits are akin to the production and consumption gains discussed in traditional theories of international trade.

On the other hand, there are potential negative fallouts for the sector and for consumers. Three major adverse consequences have been noted in the literature. The first relates to displacement of domestic professionals and firms. Due to inadequacies in quality, availability of resources and restrictive regulations affecting operations, local professionals may not be able to compete with big players in the profession and may be displaced by competition from foreign professionals. The case of accountancy has often been cited as an example, where a few large accounting firms dominate the global market and given their market power due to their staff strength, clientele, revenues, economies of scale, and global presence, have been able to displace smaller firms in domestic markets. The second adverse consequence is the reverse transfer of technology. Liberalization could lead to brain drain as the entry of foreign professional services firms makes it easier for developing country professionals to migrate and take up employment at higher wages in advanced countries. Not only does this involve a loss of the best and the brightest professionals but also amounts to subsidizing the education of professionals in advanced countries. The third negative consequence is the creation of a dual internal labor market. It has been noted in some studies that with the liberalization of professional services, firms may offer special privileges and higher compensation packages to foreign professionals and to the cream among the local professionals. They could induce the best to move out of the domestic firms to join foreign firms. This creates a two-tier structure of compensation in the profession and can raise the costs of operation and create problems of retention for domestic firms. Other adverse effects have also been cited in studies. For instance, if foreign providers receive a premium fee over the prevailing market rates due to their larger size and reputation effects, then there may be an adverse effect on the earnings of domestic firms. Market segmentation due to cream skimming could arise wherein foreign professional services firms and the higher quality domestic professional services firms cater to foreign clients and the high-paying domestic clients following the opening up of the sector while the lower quality professional service firms are left to cater to client segments such as small and medium enterprises (SMEs) and individuals.

As these opposing views on liberalization and its consequences for professional services indicate that much of the debate is perception and ideology driven, and country and sector-specific circumstances are likely to dictate the final outcome. For instance, in countries where there are numerous regulatory restrictions on the operations of domestic firms, the argument of being at a disadvantage following entry of foreign professionals who are not subject to similar restrictions is likely to be a stronger. Likewise, in professional services where the market is highly concentrated, such as in accountancy services, or where incumbency advantages based on clientele and reputation effects are very strong, the arguments of market segmentation and dual internal labor markets are likely to be important. In addition, the state of domestic firms in terms of their competitiveness, scale, capacity, standards, specialization, reputation, proximity to customers, and other such conditions are likely to influence the outcome of liberalization. Overall, one cannot say a priori whether liberalization would be beneficial or not as it is likely to be highly context-dependent. An important issue to recognize is the role regulations play in shaping the consequences of liberalization in professional services. Regulations on entry, advertising, promotion of competition, fees, and organizational form, which are common to professional services, although justifiable on grounds of consumer protection or the need to ensure competency and quality, may create competitive disadvantages for domestic firms by affecting their growth, scope of activities, and their ability to collaborate with foreign providers and raise standards. Hence, it becomes imperative to examine country and sector-specific regulatory conditions and market structure, and to solicit stakeholder views to both understand and validate the concerns and sensitivities regarding the liberalization and regulation of professional services, as this book attempts to do for the case of legal services in India.

Why Legal Services?

The legal services sector occupies a special place among professional services given its highly context-dependent nature and some of its distinctive characteristics. Among studies on professional services, those on legal services in particular are replete with references to the unique structure and values that characterize this profession and the vital role played by local systems, constitutional frameworks, and standards that set it apart from other professions which are less nationally embedded. While certain values such as independence of legal opinion and of individual lawyers, self-governance of the profession, maintaining client confidentiality, and strict standards to avoid conflicts of interest are seen as being shared globally by the legal profession, at the same time, legal professionals and associations repeatedly highlight the fact that education, practical training, and other qualifications are highly customized in this profession to suit national and local jurisdictions, what is termed "heterogeneity of substantive knowledge". Unlike in medicine or engineering where the principles are uniform across countries or in accounting where there are internationally accepted rules of practice, in law, legal training and practice varies a lot across jurisdictions and is seen as an expression of social mores and client expectations, thus having considerably more social and cultural content than other professions. Hence, it is commonly argued that this sector cannot be harmonized and regulated in the same way as many other professions, and that its commercialization through trade and investment and its treatment as a business is not desirable. Hence, there is a widespread perception in the legal fraternity that development of uniform international standards is both difficult and inappropriate. In discussions on professional services, legal services generally stand out in terms of the arguments advanced against opening up and the importance given to self-regulation.[4]

The choice of legal services is also prompted by other considerations. The sector exhibits interesting conflicts of interest regarding globalization. On the one hand, the legal fraternity, especially in the developed countries, opposes the influence of governments in negotiating protocols that would govern lawyers and their regulators under forums such as the GATS and other trade agreements. On the other hand, this same fraternity also desires enhanced trade and opening up in other markets to enhance business opportunities while protecting the domestic franchise. There are, thus, inherent assumptions in this sector regarding the role of regulators and the immunity of this profession from liberalization, which need to be examined.

In addition to these features, certain developments necessitate a closer look at legal services. One such noteworthy development is the emergence of the service providers paradigm in the legal profession, wherein the profession is not seen as a separate

---

[4] See Silver (2010 and 2000), Terry (2009), Stephen and Burns (2007), Paton (2003), and Wilkins (1992) for discussions specific to legal services.

unique profession that should be governed by its own individual regulations but rather is included under a broader class of service providers, governed by certain common principles and practices, thus justifying a common approach to their regulation. Discussions on domestic regulation under the GATS are an illustration of this widening of the service providers paradigm to include legal services. Such a paradigm shift has regulatory implications for the legal profession in terms of who should regulate the profession and how it is to be regulated.

Thus, legal services provide a good sectorial case study for re-examining the role of regulation and the impact of liberalization in professional services and specifically how the challenges of jurisdiction and autonomy of regulators are to be addressed in light of globalization. The discussion in the next chapter outlines recent and earlier trends in the globalization of legal services and key developments in this sector. The concepts and debates highlighted in this chapter provide the broader framework for analyzing these developments and trends.

2
Trade in Legal Services: Past and Present Trends

The legal services sector has experienced steady and continuous growth worldwide in the past decades. This growth has mainly been driven by international trade and business flows and the emergence of transnational firms which require supporting legal services. New fields of practice, particularly, in the area of business law have emerged owing to the rising demand for more sophisticated legal services. Growth in legal services has been particularly visible over the past decade as more and more economies have embraced globalization and opened up their economies, which has resulted in increased trade as well as capital and labor flows. Increased factor mobility and faster economic growth in many countries have led to greater demand for legal services and have thus contributed to the growth of legal services over the past decade.

Notwithstanding this growth, there are active debates surrounding the advantages and disadvantages of liberalizing legal services in both developed and developing countries. The US and the European Union (EU) are the pioneers of discussions pertaining to the opening up of legal services in their respective markets. Such debates over liberalization of legal services can be traced back first to the NAFTA negotiations and then to the GATS negotiations. In recent time also, legal services have emerged among the most important business services that are being discussed and negotiated in bilateral and plurilateral trade negotiations.

History of Legal Services Liberalization[1]

The globalization of legal services has been a subject of considerable study, discussion, and research over the last two decades. Since the end of World War II, economic and political events have propelled the globalization of law firms and thereby contributed to increased international trade in legal services. Increased globalization has also affected the domestic regulatory frameworks in the trading economies as legal professionals of two or more legal systems have been increasingly interacting with each other. Chapman and Tauber (1995) note that as and when opportunities have arisen, law firms have responded to such opportunities. They substantiate this point by noting that the first entry of the US lawyers to the European market closely followed the enactment of the Marshall Plan. Similarly, many US firms opened branch offices in London and Paris after the creation of financial institutions, such as the Eurobond and Eurodollar markets in the 1960s and 1970s.

During the past three decades, two important events, namely, NAFTA and GATS have contributed significantly to international trade in legal services. The following sections highlight how these two agreements contributed to the opening up of legal services first in the US and the EU, and later on in other parts of the globe.

NAFTA and Legal Services Liberalization

NAFTA, which was signed among the US, Canada, and Mexico, came into force on January 1, 1994. NAFTA has a chapter on trade in services establishing principles to ensure that cross-border trade in services among the three parties to the agreement is conducted in a nondiscriminatory manner. Legal services are a part of this services chapter which covers virtually all services except international air transportation and related services. The chapter on trade in services states that each party shall endeavor to ensure that its requirements

---

[1] The discussion in this section is based on Chapman and Tauber (1995).

for licensing and certifying nationals of the other parties do not constitute unnecessary barriers to trade. Moreover, the requirements should be based on objective and transparent criteria, such as competence and ability to perform a service, and they should not be more burdensome than necessary to ensure the quality of the service. The chapter also describes steps to be taken by the parties to develop mutually acceptable professional standards, and contains specific provisions relating to legal, engineering, and bus and truck transportation services. It is to be noted that NAFTA did not contain binding provisions for the mutual recognition of qualifications among the three parties. However, the agreement has specific provisions for foreign legal consultants (FLCs) to facilitate their practice among the member countries, on the basis of temporary licenses and subject to meeting certain conditions.

While the NAFTA negotiations were in progress, the US law firms realized the potential opportunities from this agreement and started spreading out their offices in Canada and Mexico. According to Goldberg (1994), the negotiations and subsequent implementation of NAFTA prompted the US law firms to open three offices in Canada and 11 in Mexico, thereby a total of 14 new offices between 1988 and 1993. As a consequence, between 1988 and 1993, the US exports of legal services to Canada increased from US$20 to US$97 million, while exports to Mexico grew from US$1 to US$19 million (Chapman and Tauber 1995). Thus, total trade in legal services between the US and its NAFTA partners expanded significantly as a result of the agreement. With this increase in legal services trade within the region, issues pertaining to the opening up of legal services and elimination of regulatory barriers on practice, licensing, and entry of foreign law firms (FLFs) in these markets became the center point of discussions.

Although NAFTA negotiations and the implementation of this agreement contributed to the globalization of legal services within the North American region, law firms based in other countries did not remain untouched. In order to compete internationally, non-US firms, especially from large commercial centers, recognized that they had to adopt international practices (as followed by the US firms), including opening up offices in other countries' jurisdictions. Thus, many European firms started new offices in the US and Asian legal markets. As a consequence, both the North American and European markets have witnessed a concentration of large law firms over the last 20 years.

GATS and Legal Services Liberalization[2]

The GATS is an integral part of the WTO that came into existence in January 1995 as a result of the Uruguay Round negotiations. The GATS extends the multilateral trading system to the service sector in the same way as the General Agreement on Tariffs and Trade (GATT) provides for merchandise trade. All members of the WTO are signatories to the GATS. The GATS classifies services into 12 major categories, with more than 161 subsectors across these 12 sectors. Legal services are included in the subcategory of professional services under the broad category of business services.

During the Uruguay Round, the WTO Secretariat released a note titled 'Trade in Professional Services'. This note focused on licensed professions, including law, architecture, accounting, and medicine. The objective was to identify core issues of relevance to these different sectors, and to raise questions concerning barriers to trade in these services. As licensing and qualification requirements are the two most important barriers to trade in legal services, the willingness to engage on these issues during the GATS negotiations signaled the need to reduce barriers to legal practice which were common across jurisdictions. In July 1998, the WTO Secretariat released a background note on legal services to provide background information on the legal services sector and to facilitate discussion in the Council for Trade in Services of the WTO on the exchange of information program. The note tracked the growth of international trade in legal services and attributed it to both demand and supply side factors. The demand

---

[2] The discussion in this section is based on Paton (2003).

side arguments included the internationalization of the economy and the consequent client demand for lawyers to address transactional needs; interest in 'one stop shopping'; and access to high-quality services, on the one hand. On the other hand, supply side arguments related to the view of certain countries that the establishment of foreign lawyers is a catalyst for foreign investment. The note identified business law and international law as the sectors most affected by international trade in legal services. However, it also warned that "the entry of foreign service suppliers in the more traditional sectors of domestic law should not be completely discounted as the sector becomes increasingly more integrated and competitive".³

The note flagged various regulatory barriers to trade in legal services. These included market access barriers such as nationality requirements, restrictions on movement of professionals, prohibitions on incorporation, and other restrictions on legal form. It also identified national treatment limitations such as restrictions on partnership with local professionals, rules on the use of international and foreign firm names, residency requirements, and general discrimination in the hiring process. According to the note, qualification requirements often represent an insurmountable barrier to trade in legal services, especially for the practice of host country law. The note also refers to FLCs, i.e., professionals practicing international, home, and third-country laws, and the fact that although these professionals are subject to qualification-related barriers while rendering cross-border services, they still remain subject to numerous other unnecessary and burdensome domestic regulations in most WTO Member countries.

Thus, it could be argued that both NAFTA and GATS laid the background for the globalization of legal services. While neither of these agreements has been able to address the wide range of regulatory barriers affecting legal services trade, they are seminal agreements in that they contain important provisions and provide a framework for future liberalization in this sector. There is also

---

³ See WTO Background Note on Legal Services (1998).

evidence from other regions to indicate the scope for liberalizing legal services. For instance, three EU Directives on qualification requirements showed that deeper integration could be achieved through the mutual recognition of qualifications, full integration into the legal profession of a host state, and a more liberal approach.

GATS Classification of Legal Services and Existing Commitments[4]

As legal systems differ from one country to another, defining 'legal services' is very important for trade negotiation purposes. As mentioned earlier, the WTO 'Services Sectoral Classification List' puts legal services as a subsector of 'professional services' under 'business services'. This entry corresponds to the central product classification (CPC) number 861 in the United Nations provisional central product classification (UNCPC) of 1991. The WTO classification does not provide any further subcategories of legal services. However, the UNCPC further subdivides legal services (861) into legal advisory and representation services concerning criminal law (CPC 86111); legal advisory and representation services in judicial procedures concerning other fields of law (CPC 86119); legal advisory and representation services in statutory procedures of quasi-judicial tribunals, boards, etc. (CPC 86120); legal documentation and certification services (CPC 86130); and other legal advisory and information services (CPC 86190).

Legal advisory and representation services concerning criminal law (CPC 86111) include legal advisory and representation services during the litigation process, and drafting services of legal documentation in relation to criminal law. Generally, this implies the defense of a client in front of a judicial body in a case of criminal offence. However, it can also consist of acting as a prosecutor in a case of criminal offence when private legal practitioners are hired on

---

[4] Based on the background note on legal services of WTO (2010).

a fee basis by the government. Both the pleading of a case in court and out-of-court legal work are included. The latter comprises research and other work for the preparation of a criminal case (e.g., researching legal documentation, interviewing witnesses, reviewing police and other reports), and the execution of post-litigation work, in relation to criminal law.

Legal advisory and representation services in judicial procedures concerning other fields of law (CPC 86119) consist of legal advisory and representation services during the litigation process, and drafting services of legal documentation in relation to law other than criminal law. Representation services generally consist of either acting as a prosecutor on behalf of the client, or defending the client from a prosecution. This category also includes both the pleading of a case in court, and out-of-court legal work.

Legal advisory and representation services in statutory procedures of quasi-judicial tribunals, boards, etc. (CPC 86120), include legal advisory and representation services during the litigation process, and drafting services of legal documentation in relation to statutory procedures. Generally, this implies the representation of a client in front of a statutory body (e.g., an administrative tribunal). Both the pleading of a case in front of authorized bodies other than judicial courts and the related legal work are included in this category. The latter comprises research and other work for the preparation of a nonjudicial case (e.g., researching legal documentation, interviewing witnesses, and reviewing reports) and the execution of post-litigation work.

The legal documentation and certification services (CPC 86130) category pertains to preparation, drawing up, and certification services of legal documents. The services generally comprise the provision of a number of related legal services, including the provision of advice and the execution of various tasks necessary for the drawing up or certification of documents, such as wills, marriage contracts, commercial contracts, business charters, etc.

Other legal advisory and information services (CPC 86190) include advisory services to clients related to their legal rights and obligations and providing information on legal matters not elsewhere classified. For instance, services such as escrow services and estate settlement services are included under this category.

Post-1997 versions of the CPC also include 'arbitration and conciliation services' as a subclass of legal services. It is interesting to note that rather than adopting these distinctions for undertaking commitments under the GATS, a number of member states have scheduled GATS commitments in a different way on the ground that the above-mentioned classification does not represent the actual way in which trade in legal services takes place. They have instead adopted the following categories: host country law (advisory/representation), home country law and/or third-country law (advisory/representation), international law (advisory/representation), legal documentation and certification services, and other advisory and information services.

As far as commitments are concerned, according to the 2010 background note on legal services, 76 members have taken commitments in legal services under the GATS. As indicated earlier, only 13 members have used the classification contained in W/120, referring to the CPC 861, without any modifications. Three members have made commitments on legal services without any reference to the CPC. The most common departure from the classification in W/120 and the CPC is the limitation of the commitments to advisory/consultancy services on home country (i.e., foreign) law, and international law and the exclusion of services in host country (i.e., domestic) law.

The largest number of commitments exists in advisory services in home country law, where 69 members made at least partial commitments for cross-border supply (Mode 1), and 68 for commercial presence (Mode 3).[5] There are considerably fewer commitments on

---

[5] According to the WTO GATS terminology, Mode 1 refers to cross-border trade in services (such as telemedicine, BPO), Mode 2 refers to consumption abroad (such as medical treatment or education in other countries), Mode 3 refers to commercial presence (such as foreign banks in the home country), and Mode 4 refers to temporary movement of natural persons (such as nurses or IT professionals' movement to overseas country) to provide their services.

the practice of the law of the host jurisdiction. Twenty-eight members scheduled commitments on advisory services in host country law for cross-border supply, and 29 for commercial presence. Slightly fewer commitments still have been made for representation services in host country law, with 25 commitments for Mode 1 and 27 for Mode 3. Commitments in international law typically follow those for foreign law. Sixty-eight members have made commitments on Mode 1 and 67 for Mode 3. Specific commitments for the movement of natural persons (Mode 4) are governed, with very few exceptions, by referral to the horizontal section of members' schedules. Thus, as is evident, countries have been more conservative with respect to host country law and on commercial presence. As is the case across all services under the GATS, cross-border mobility of service providers in this profession has not been liberalized.

International Trade in Legal Services: Present Status

With the continuous rise in international transactions owing to more and more cross-border business activities in recent years, law firms have expanded their operations globally by establishing their offices in other countries, such as China, Russia, and other fast growing emerging markets. These law firms are providing expert legal advice not only in traditional business activities, such as corporate restructuring, cross-border mergers and acquisitions, etc., but also in new and emerging areas, such as intellectual property rights (IPR), new financial instruments and competition law, outsourcing, etc.

As these services are becoming global day by day, there is an emerging need to adapt the regulatory environment for these services to keep pace with the evolving nature of business activities and to protect consumers. Countries are also increasingly feeling the need to draw upon global best practices in this sector in order to modify their national frameworks, in order to be competitive, build capacity, and ensure sustained growth in the sector.

Market Size

With the growing importance of the service sector in general and with technological developments such as new transmission technologies, the 'trade ability' of legal services has increased over the years. According to the Datamonitor (2014) research report *Legal Services: Global Industry Guide*, the global legal services market had total revenues of US$610.4 billion in 2013, representing a compound annual growth rate (CAGR) of 3 percent between 2009 and 2013. In comparison, the US, the European, and Asia-Pacific markets registered CAGRs of 1.4 percent, 3.2 percent, and 5.9 percent, respectively, over the same period, to reach respective values of US$275.8 billion, US$184.5 billion, and US$80.4 billion in 2013, as shown in Figure 2.1.

A segmentation of the legal services market by geographic region shows that the US accounts for 45 percent of services, followed by Europe (30 percent), and Asia-Pacific (13 percent) in 2013. The corresponding figures for 2010 were 54 percent, 33 percent, and 12 percent, respectively, as shown in Figure 2.2 (Datamonitor 2014).

A comparison of market segmentation in 2010 and 2013 shows that market shares of the US and the EU have come down over

Figure 2.1
The Legal Services Market in the US, Europe, Asia-Pacific, and the World, 2013

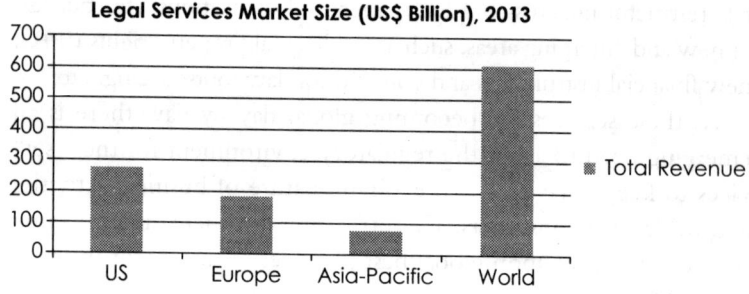

Source: Datamonitor (2014).

Figure 2.2
Global Legal Services Market Segmentation, 2013 and 2010

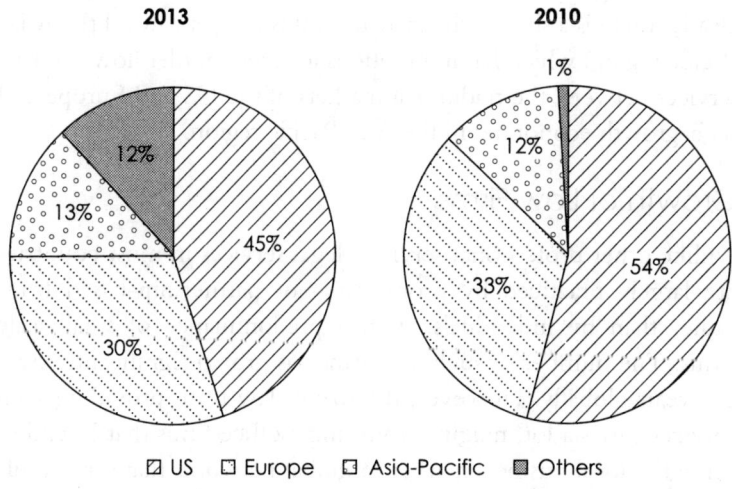

Source: Datamonitor (2014).

this period whereas the shares of the Asia Pacific and others have increased. This is a reflection of the growing role of emerging economies in the global legal services market. The market is forecast to grow further, with an anticipated CAGR of 4.2 percent for the 2013–2018 period and a projected market value of US$750.9 billion by the end of 2018. Comparatively, the US, European, and the Asia-Pacific markets are projected to register CAGRs of 3.1 percent, 3.6 percent, and 7 percent, respectively, over the same period and to reach respective values of 321.9 billion, US$220.2 billion, and US$112.9 billion by the end of 2018 (Datamonitor 2014).

The number of legal professionals has also increased, recording a CAGR of 2.7 percent between 2009 and 2013, reaching a total of 4082.1 thousand legal professionals in 2013. The US market volume registered a CAGR of 1.5 percent between 2009 and 2013 to reach a total of 1,278.8 thousand legal professionals in 2013, while the Europe market volume witnessed a CAGR of 2.4 percent between 2009 and 2013 to reach a total of 1,141.3 thousand legal professionals in 2013. The Asia-Pacific market volume increased with a

CAGR of 6.9 percent over the same period to reach a total of 496.4 thousand legal professionals in 2013 (Datamonitor 2014). Thus, clearly, there is a shift in the growth of this market toward the Asia-Pacific region, which has implications for cross-border flows of legal services between the traditional markets of the US and Europe and high-growth economies in the Asia-Pacific region.

Growth of Law Firms

Unlike other professional services, legal services in most countries are largely practiced by proprietary- or partnership-based firms rather than by individuals, with a predominance of small-scale firms. The number of such law firms has grown significantly over the years globally. However, the size of law firms providing such services varies a lot, ranging from single office firms that intend to serve the local business market to global networks that serve multinational organizations.

According to the 2010 background note on legal services of the WTO, the legal services sector has experienced significant growth in revenues and consolidation over the past decade. This has resulted in the creation of a growing number of multinational law firms with vastly increased numbers of lawyers. An overview of the largest law firms ranked by the number of lawyers shows a clear nexus between the size of the company and the internationalization of practice. The top ten firms have offices in more than ten countries, and seven of them have more than 60 percent of their lawyers outside the home office. Moreover, the overall number of lawyers employed by the top-ranking firms has risen sharply. There is a high concentration of the major law firms among the developed countries. Ranked by revenue, 74 of the top 100 law firms were from the US, followed by the UK (14) and Australia (5). Figure 2.3 shows the growth of top 50 law firms over the period 1998–1999 and 2007–2008.

Table 2.1 provides the top ranked 20 law firms based on the market rankings by Acritas Sharplegal (2014) Global Elite Brand Index. This index evaluated firms based on awareness, favorability, and consideration for multi-jurisdictional litigation and deals.

Figure 2.3
Percentage Growth of Top 50 Legal Firms, 1998/99–2007/08

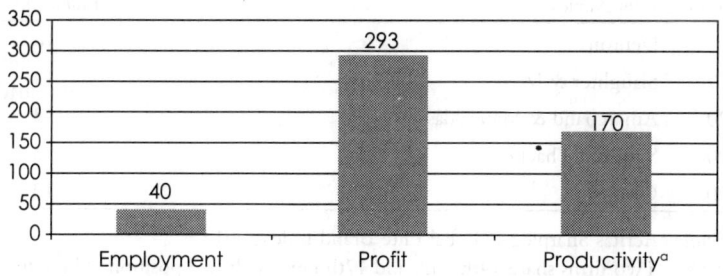

Source: Reproduced from the background note on legal services, WTO Secretariat (2010), p. 4.
Note: [a] Profit/Revenue.

Table 2.1
Top Ranked 20 Law Firms

Rank	Firm Name	Brand Index
1	Baker & McKenzie	100
2	Clifford Chance	61
3	Norton Rose Fulbright	53
4	DLA Piper	48
5	Linklaters	45
6	Freshfields	44
7	Allen & Overy	42
8	Hogan Lovells	37
9	Jones Day	36
10	Skadden	32
11	Herbert Smith Freehills	29
12	White & Case	22
13	Latham & Watkins	19
14	King & Wood Mallesons	18
14	Eversheds	18
16	Sidley Austin	17
17	Reed Smith	16

(Table 2.1 Continued)

(Table 2.1 Continued)

Rank	Firm Name	Brand Index
17	Dentons	16
19	Slaughter & May	14
20	Amarchand & Mangaldas	13
20	Simpson Thacher	13
20	CMS	13

Source: Acritas Sharplegal Global Elite Brand Index, 2014.
Note: Two firms share 14th rank and 17th rank with tied position. Three firms share 20th rank with tied position.

Foreign Operations of Law Firms

The spread of international law firms over the years suggests two principal patterns of overseas expansion. First is the "follow your client" model, in which law firms expanded into foreign markets as their client companies expanded their operations to overseas countries. This client-focused expansion had taken place in the 1980s and 1990s within developed country markets, but has now spread to many developing countries having operations of multinational enterprises. It is to be noted that in this model, the law firms concerned usually deal with corporate law matters and do not engage in work in the purely domestic legal services market. A variant of the model can be seen in emerging markets like Hong Kong, China, Singapore, or the United Arab Emirates, where international law firms have created hubs from which they serve the wider regional markets.

In another business model, usually observed within developed economies, foreign-owned law firms have expanded to other countries to serve a broader range of clients, and areas of practice. For instance, in the UK, over 50 percent of the revenue of the largest 100 law firms is generated by international firms based in London. Over time, depending on the development of a market and its regulatory structure, a firm's focus may broaden from the "follow your client" model to increasingly serving the local legal services market as well.

The size of law firms also affects how law firms operate in foreign markets. While larger firms tend to establish overseas offices, smaller ones focus more on network relationships where the individual suppliers retain their respective outlooks and approaches (Silver et al. 2009).

An important recent phenomenon that has influenced the legal services landscape is outsourcing. Law firms outsource routine tasks such as document review, legal transcription, litigation support, and legal publishing services to other countries in order to reduce their operating costs. These are generally lower value tasks and do not constitute the core business of a law firm. However, it is observed that law firms having successful offshoring of lower-value tasks increasingly tend to offshore higher value tasks also.

According to the WTO Secretariat Note (2010), India is projected to become the main destination for legal services outsourcing. The estimates projected that the revenues from legal outsourcing in India would grow from US$ 146 million in 2006 to US$640 million by the end of 2010, with employment increasing from 7,500 to 32,000 over the same period (*ValueNotes Outsourcing Weekly* 2006). The main clients for outsourced legal work to India are law firms, accounting for approximately 45 percent of their offshore revenue and corporate law departments which account for another 36 percent of their revenue.

Issues in Trade in Legal Services

Though the legal profession has grown tremendously in the past few decades keeping pace with the general opening up of world economies, there are many issues and challenges that are affecting the globalization of this profession. The first challenge is due to the fact that despite the growing international presence of the law firms, most of the countries maintain various types of restrictions that affect the flow of legal services across borders. As a consequence, domestic firms find it difficult to provide their services in overseas markets.

An important issue affecting trade in legal services is recognition of foreign qualifications. Foreign degrees and credentials are generally not accepted in most of the countries and hence serve as a barrier to foreign penetration. Though, efforts have been made to conclude mutual recognition agreements (MRAs), they are far from adequate. MRAs, while offering a feasible solution to the problem associated with liberalization of legal services are subject to implementation issues. The implementation challenges relate to questions about how to bridge the gap in educational qualifications and other training requirements of professionals between the signing countries, the perceived risk of lowering the professional standards of agreeing countries by signing MRAs, and the citizenship and residency requirements in the practice of professions globally.

There are also conceptual and practical issues affecting international trade in legal services. For instance, there are different kinds of laws practiced in a country, such as home country law, host country law, third-country law, international law, etc. Many times, in the absence of clear regulatory guidelines, it becomes difficult to understand what kind of law foreign nationals are permitted to practice in a country. Under such conditions, trade in legal services becomes conceptually difficult to track and measure. Similarly, there is lack of uniformity in the classification of legal services for scheduling of commitments under the GATS. This, to some extent, undermines the value of GATS commitments in legal services.

Apart from the above issues, it needs to be noted that it is difficult to assess the value of trade in legal services as trade statistics are not available by modes of supply as outlined by the GATS. Moreover, most countries do not collect data at a sufficiently disaggregated level to separate legal from other business services. This problem is of course not specific to legal services alone but applies to the measurement of services trade more generally and affects the measurement of a wide range of increasingly tradable business and other services.

Legal Services Restrictiveness Indices

Legal services trade is not only difficult to capture in value but is also difficult to measure in terms of the level of protection. As the bulk of restrictions in legal services trade take the form of regulations at the border and behind-the-border, it is very difficult to capture the incidence of protection levels. Notwithstanding these difficulties, the OECD and the World Bank have attempted to quantify the incidence of regulatory restrictiveness affecting trade in legal services for a number of countries.

OECD Services Trade Restrictiveness Index[6]

The OECD has constructed the services trade restrictiveness index (STRI) for the 34 OECD countries and six major emerging economies (Brazil, the People's Republic of China [PRC], India, Indonesia, the Russian Federation, and South Africa) for legal services. The STRI takes values between zero and one, one being the most restrictive and zero being the most open. The STRIs are calculated on the basis of a regulatory database that contains comparable and standardized information on trade and investment related policies in force in each country.

The STRI database is based on regulations under five policy categories, namely, restrictions on foreign entry, restrictions on the movement of people, other discriminatory measures, barriers to competition, and regulatory transparency. Thus, the index goes beyond discriminatory measures and includes domestic regulations that are important for effective market access and the creation of competitive markets. These include regulations affecting competition and technical standards, as well as a range of measures related to regulatory transparency and administrative requirements.

An important characteristic of legal services is that qualification requirements are particularly stringent since the profession is divided across national lines and reflects the national character of the law. International law firms and lawyers typically enter foreign markets to practice international law, their home country law, or the law of a third country. They are not allowed to practice host country law. Many countries have introduced a limited license for legal services restricting the scope of the services that can be provided by foreign legal professionals and restricting the latter from practicing host country law. The OECD STRI focuses on the requirements

---

[6] Based on OECD Sectoral Note (2014).

for obtaining a full license to practice, though it also contains information on whether limited licensing is in place and the services that the business lawyers or law firms with a limited licence may provide. The detailed information on the regulations included in the STRI database for legal services is provided in Table A.1.

The STRI values for various countries are shown in Figure 2.4. The figure depicts the overall index for legal services, broken down by policy categories, together with a line indicating the sample average. The level of restrictiveness ranges from 0.11 to 0.73, with an average of 0.31. This overall level, while higher than in some other sectors, is lessened somewhat by the possibility of service provision in segments other than host country law.

Figure 2.4 also reveals that restrictions to movement of people contribute the most to the STRI values for most of the countries,

Figure 2.4
OECD Services Trade Restrictiveness Index (STRI) for Legal Services, 2014

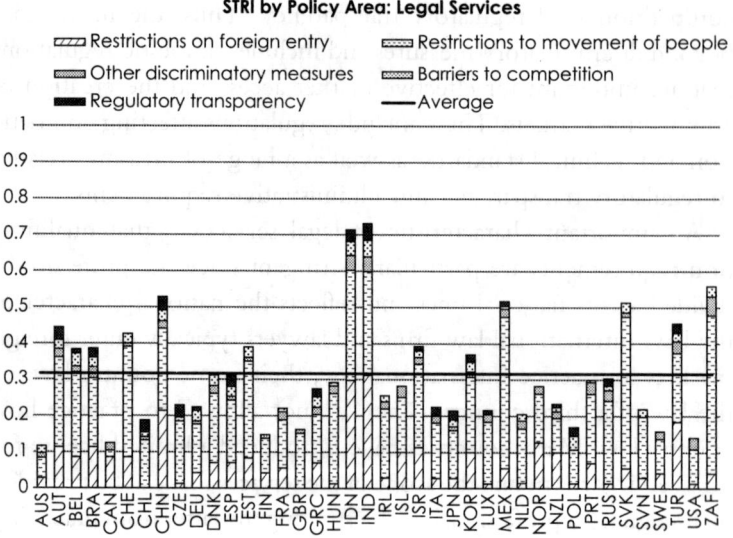

Source: Reproduced from the OECD Sectoral Note (2014), "STRI Sector Brief: Legal services", p. 1.

followed by restrictions on foreign entry. This is in part due to the characteristics of these services, which are skilled labor intensive. As mentioned earlier, the barriers facing foreign lawyers often relate to the scope of the services they may provide, recognition of the qualifications required to obtain a license, and the linking of ownership of law firms to holding a license. A number of countries limit foreign lawyers and law firms' activities to legal services in international law and their home country law.

The WTO's sectoral note on legal services suggests that easing a few prominent restrictions can result in a significantly more liberal and competitive market environment for legal services, with considerable economy wide benefits. This is particularly true for legal services considering the important role these services play in facilitating business, and as a part of the infrastructure that underpins international trade.

World Bank Restrictiveness Indices[7]

The World Bank has compiled a services trade restrictions database that provides comparable information on services trade policy measures for 103 countries for various service sectors including legal services. An interesting feature of this database is that it also provides regulatory information for key modes of delivery (Mode 1: cross-border supply, Mode 3: establishing commercial presence, and Mode 4: presence of service supplying individuals) for these services, thus enabling construction of modal restrictiveness indices for different service sectors.

The database contains policy information on individual policy measures as well as a summary of key restrictions by country, sector, and mode of delivery. In addition, the database provides a preliminary quantification of the restrictiveness of policy.

The World Bank has constructed the STRI at the most disaggregated level for any combination of subsector and mode. This

---

[7] Based on Services Trade Restriction Database of the World Bank, available at http://iresearch.worldbank.org/servicestrade/ (last accessed on January 1, 2015).

measure of openness is simple and transparent. Compared to other indices based on a fixed set of scores and weights, it avoids problems such as the double-counting of nonbinding restrictions. As compared to measures which infer restrictiveness through the impact of measures on some outcome, this measure is not dependent on the availability of data on services sector performance.

Within each subsector mode, the policy regimes are assessed in their entirety, and the bundle of applied policies is mapped into five broad categories (with associated scores): completely open (0); virtually open but with minor restrictions (25); major restrictions (50); virtually closed with limited opportunities to enter and operate (75); and completely closed (100).

Table 2.2 and Figure 2.5 present overall and modal STRI for legal services across the selected countries in 2010. The detailed information on these regulations is available in Table A.2.

Figure 2.5 and Table 2.2 indicate wide variation in opening up of legal services across countries. While Australia has an open environment across all modes, India has the most restrictive regulatory environment. If we compare across the modes, Mode 4 is generally the most restricted mode in all the countries, followed by Mode 3. The OECD STRI also reflected restrictions on the movement of people as the most important regulations across countries.

Table 2.2

World Bank Overall and Modal Restrictiveness Indices for Legal Services, 2010

Country	Overall	Mode 1	Mode 3	Mode 4
Australia	35	0	25	50
China	80	0	83.33	83.33
India	85.8	100	100	66.67
Japan	53.3	100	50	50
Malaysia	81.7	0	75	100
UK	41.7	25	16.67	66.67
USA	55	0	50	66.67

Source: STRI Database of the World Bank.

Figure 2.5
World Bank Overall and Modal Restrictiveness Indices for Legal Services, 2010

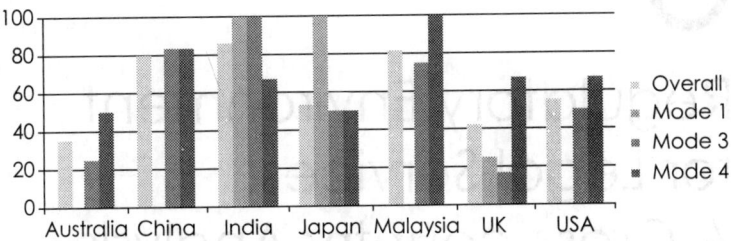

Source: STRI Database of the World Bank.

Overall, across the various kinds of restrictiveness indicators available for legal services, it is evident that the sector is subject to numerous regulatory measures, at the border and behind-the-border. There are also considerable differences across countries in the application of these measures. But the general pattern that emerges is that restrictions on the mobility of providers and restrictions on foreign entry constitute the bulk of measures affecting legal services, with developing countries exhibiting higher entry barriers and developed countries applying more restrictions on professional mobility in this sector. Thus, there is an interesting complementarity of interest evident in these measures, in that developing countries are more likely to want access to other markets for their professionals, while developed countries are more likely to push for the establishment of their law firms in other markets. Such issues, as seen later in this book, very much characterize the nature of the debate over deregulating and liberalizing legal services in India.

3

Regulatory Environment for Legal Services: A Cross-country Analysis

As outlined in the first chapter, legal services are one of the most important professional services having many unique characteristics. World over legal services are one of the most protected services segments. Because of the inherent problem of information asymmetry and consequent market failures, legal services are subject to a number of restrictions across the globe. It is worth noting that many of these restrictions could be regarded as anticompetitive, but at the same time these are justified as they are aimed at protecting public interest.

Regulatory Framework for Legal Services[1]

There exist four important regulations that restrict the provision of legal services in a country but which are justified on the grounds of public interest. These are: restrictions on entry, restrictions on advertising and promotion of competition, regulation of fees, and restrictions on organizational form. Restrictions on fee,

---

[1] The discussion in this section is based on Stephen and Burns (2007).

advertising, and organizational form tend to limit the means by which members of the legal profession can compete with each other. For instance, a new supplier of legal services may find it difficult to tap the potential clients due to restrictions on advertising. Such restrictions on advertising can also increase the search costs for the consumers and hence they tend to stick to the existing service providers. These restrictions combined with fee restrictions make the option of choosing between service providers irrelevant for the consumers. This could have serious implications for the sector as a whole in the long run as in the absence of competition and market pressure to innovate, the existing service providers are more likely to follow the routine systems and processes and the growth, strength, and competitiveness of the sector could be adversely affected in the long run.

Restrictions on Entry

Entry into the market for legal services could be restricted in two ways: First, only the persons holding certain qualifications and membership of specified bodies have the right to provide certain services. These may be referred to as professional monopoly rights. Second, entry to these professional bodies themselves may be subject to restriction. Economists are critical of restrictions on entry into a profession as economic theory suggests that entry restrictions lead to supply shortages which allow members of that profession to earn economic rents. According to Stephen and Love (2000), "The monopoly right ensures that an adjustment in supply from outside the profession cannot take place in response to the profession's high incomes."

Theory of competition states that if super normal profits exist in a normal business, other players enter the market thereby increasing the available quantity and reducing the price. Thus, excess demand is met by the offerings of the new entrants and ultimately the super normal profits vanish and all service providers earn normal profits. However, this may not happen in the case of legal services as there are strict entry barriers which prevent new entrants from entering the market. Thus, the existing service players continue to extract super normal profit.

Though monopoly rights in principle lead to economic rents causing a market failure, it is also important to note that there is a tradeoff between competition and quality. While relaxing entry requirements could help in increasing competition, it could also lead to a reduction in standards below the socially optimal level. On the other hand, very stringent entry requirements may help in maintaining the desired level of quality but may reduce the level of competition. Thus, an important challenge before the regulatory bodies and policy makers is to strike a right balance between competition and quality in the provision of legal services.

It is unclear in the literature how monopoly rights affect competition in the legal services market. Shaked and Sutton (1981) were of the opinion that monopolistic powers available to service providers in self-regulating professions are likely to reduce welfare and that allowing the entry of rival para-professions could improve welfare. Ogus (1995) suggests the presence of more than one professional body in order to solve the problem of monopoly rights created by self-regulation. Establishment of more than one professional body in self-regulated professions such as legal services would enable competition and quality to exist simultaneously as these professional bodies are likely to compete with each other in enforcing regulatory standards. However, having more than one professional body may also lead to the problem of control and coordination among these bodies.

Regulation on Advertising

Advertising serves as an important means to reduce the problem of information asymmetry in any professional service, including legal services. Information asymmetry can be reduced by using traditional sources of information and/or modern methods of communications. Hudec and Trebilcock (1982) suggest various traditional sources of information available to consumers of legal services. These include personal experiences gained from general knowledge or previous employment of a lawyer; recommendations from friends, business acquaintances, and family members; social contacts with lawyers; initial consultation with a lawyer; recommendations from agencies such as law society referral services, legal aid or the ombudsman; entries in the Yellow Pages and the like; and public legal education and collective advertising. They are of the opinion that none of these sources meet the necessary criteria of expertise, breadth of information, objectivity, and low cost.

Advertising is a modern method of reducing information asymmetry. It could be an important source of information for the consumers of legal services and could help them significantly in making informed decisions. Advertising could lead to improved information flows, reduced search costs, reduced setup time and costs for consumers, innovation and creation of innovative practices, and product differentiation. However, it is not free from weaknesses, including difficulty in discerning the truthfulness of any claims made, unsuitability of many areas of law for advertising, and raising entry costs.

Advertising is one of the areas most affected by the deregulation wave in the past two decades across the globe. It is also one of the most studied aspects of legal services regulations. Love and Stephen (1996) analyze empirical evidence on the effects of advertising in professional service markets. All except one study suggest an association between advertising and lower fees for professional services, though these studies are subject to limitations in their empirical methodology. Some studies compare the fees of advertising firms with those of non-advertising firms. The evidence from the available literature generally supports the view that more advertising in a market leads to lower fees in that market. Schroeter et al. (1987) are of the opinion that advertising increases competition amongst sellers in a market and thus helps make the representative firm's demand curve more elastic.

Regulation of Fees

Regulations on fees, such a mandatory fixed fees and setting of fee caps, can be very restrictive. Some studies argue that fees could be decided by the competitive forces of the market. There is some deregulation in this context. While traditionally, fees were controlled via mandated fee scales, over a period of time, these have gradually been converted into 'recommended' fees.

One of the important uses of having fee regulations is to mitigate the adverse selection problem arising from information asymmetry. Fee schedules can act as a useful source of information for consumers as they are aware of the cost of a service before the consumption of that service. However, the regulation of fees does not guarantee the quality of legal service; rather it only guarantees the cost to be paid by the consumers for a particular service. Van Den Bergh (2006) argues that fee regulations can be used to keep up quality as the promise of high incomes will encourage high-quality service providers to enter the market.

As the information on actual fees that deviate from mandatory fee scales is difficult to obtain, not much empirical research has been done on the impact of fee regulations. Arnould and Friedland (1976) based on their study of America concluded that lawyers' incomes were higher where fee schedules existed, and prohibiting the use of fee schedules by the government is an appropriate policy response to improving competition in legal service markets.

Restrictions on Organizational Form

Almost all countries put restrictions on the form of organization for the legal practitioners. The allowed forms of practicing range from sole proprietorship to partnership firms with limited or unlimited liability to corporate form. The restriction could also take the form in which the members of the profession are allowed to form partnership with nonmembers. In general, nonlawyers are not permitted to own a law firm except a few cases wherein nonlawyer ownership of law firms is permitted. For instance, New South Wales (NSW) in Australia allows nonlawyer ownership of law firms.

Practicing through partnership offers many benefits to the legal service providers. These include economies of scale, economies of specialization, economies of scope, and risk spreading. Economies of scale occur when the fixed costs of producing a good or service are spread over greater volumes of output. Thus, the average fixed cost per unit output comes down with the increase in output. Though legal services do not involve high capital investment as most of the investment in such services is in the form of human capital, economies of scale may still be relevant and can be possible through sharing of support staff, library facilities, computer systems, and advertising expenditure.

Economies of specialization occur when specialists become more proficient than nonspecialists in their area of specialization. This could happen in legal services if the specialist lawyers dealing in particular laws become more proficient than the generalist or nonspecialist lawyers. Economies of specialization have twin advantages of reducing costs and improving quality. It is worth noting that though sole practitioners can also have economies of specialization, they may not be able to have varied economies of specialization required at different points of time. There is also a tradeoff between economies of specialization and risk spreading. If a sole practitioner opts for becoming a specialist, he/she increases the risk of getting adequate work as the demand for the specialization may not remain uniform all the time. However, if he/she opts to become a generalist, then he/she may get adequate work throughout the year though realization of economies of specialization may not be possible. Consequently, sole practitioners are less likely to be specialists than lawyers working in a large group practice. On the other hand, large firms are likely to have economies of specialization as their risk is spread on account of the multiplicity of lawyers.

Economies of scope are realized when the cost of providing more than one service within a single firm is less than the cost of each service being provided by different firms. One can understand that whereas for sole practitioners economies of scope would lead to reduced economies of specialization, group practice can potentially capture both economies of scope and economies of specialization. It is this combination of economies of scope and specialization that is used to justify the case for multidisciplinary partnerships (MDPs).

Apart from the restrictions on organizational forms, restrictions could also be on the form of practice. Accordingly, legal practitioners are divided into two kinds of professions: those who appear before the courts and others who provide legal advice to clients. The former category is generally called 'advocate' whereas the latter is considered as 'solicitors'.

Regulatory Environment in Selected Countries

This section provides an overview of the key aspects of regulations prevailing in the legal services sector for a selected set of countries and presents some observations and inferences regarding cross-country regulatory practices in this sector. The countries selected include Australia, China, Malaysia, Japan, Singapore, the UK, and the US. The choice of these countries is motivated by the fact that they provide a good mix in terms of characteristics such as language, legal system, stage of development, market size, and degree of restrictiveness and openness.

The regulatory aspects selected for discussion include the legal system, the regulatory framework, practice requirements, mode of practice, entry requirements for foreign lawyers, insurance requirements, advertising, and FDI regulations. These aspects were selected on the basis of a review of the literature on regulations in the legal profession (some of which were discussed in the previous section) as well as insights gained from discussions with practitioners and regulators in this sector.

Legal Systems

An analysis of the legal systems for the selected set of countries reveals that the legal systems in these countries fall into three main categories: civil law, common law, and mixed or pluralistic law. The difference between civil law and common law lies in the source of authority. While the main source of authority is case law in the form of judicial opinions in common law countries, in civil law countries, codified laws predominate. Apart from this, in common law countries, judges act as arbitrators, presiding over lawyer-led proceedings, and fashioning appropriate remedies somewhat flexibly. In civil law countries, however, judges have a more central role, investigating facts, examining witnesses, and applying codified law to their findings in a somewhat stricter manner than in common law countries.[2]

Australia, Singapore, and the US have legal systems based on common law. Malaysia has a common law system based on a mixture of case law and statute law. Muslims in Malaysia are also governed by Islamic law, which is administered by the Sharia Courts for personal matters, including those relating to marriage, divorce, division or disposition of matrimonial property, inheritance, and personal conduct in breach of Islamic law (e.g., indecent dressing).[3]

China has a socialist legal system based on the civil law model. It does not have an independent judiciary or a legal system that operates outside the influence of the ruling party.[4] Japan has a civil law system which is largely based on the German legal system with some influence from French law. It is also heavily influenced in specific areas of law (such as corporations and securities law) by American common law. The UK has three legal systems. While English law, which applies in England and Wales, and Northern Ireland law, which applies in Northern Ireland, are based on common-law principles, Scots law, which applies in Scotland, is a pluralistic system based on civil law principles with some elements of common law.[5]

Regulatory Frameworks

Analysis of the regulatory frameworks applicable for legal profession in the selected set of countries reveals that the legal profession in these countries is either 'unified' or 'fused'. The 'unified' legal

---

[2] See http://onlinelaw.wustl.edu/major-differences-between-the-japanese-and-american-legal-systems/ (last accessed January 1, 2015).

[3] See http://www.muslim-lawyers.net/news/datoothman.html (last accessed on January 1, 2015).

[4] See http://worldsavvy.org/monitor/index.php?option=com_content&view=article&id=113:legal-system&catid=54:keyplayersinternal&Itemid=176

[5] See http://en.wikipedia.org/wiki/Law_of_the_United_Kingdom (last accessed on January 1, 2015).

profession means that there is only a single class of legal professionals such as the advocates. On the other hand, the 'fused' legal profession means that the legal professionals can work either as solicitors or as advocates.

In Australia, the legal profession is split in each state between barrister and solicitor, but it is not very pronounced. Solicitors are regulated at the state level by law societies and must belong to a state professional body (i.e., Law Society) in order to be permitted to practice. At the federal level, there is an overarching legal system consisting of federal courts, and a solicitor admitted to a state jurisdiction can practice at a federal level. In some jurisdictions, lawyers can practice as both barristers and solicitors, but in others, the traditional separation between barristers (advocates) and solicitors remains.[6]

In China, the legal profession is unified. On the other hand, legal professionals in Japan are mainly divided into two branches—barristers and scrivener (means solicitor). There are also two kinds of scriveners: administrative scriveners and judicial scriveners.[7]

The legal profession in Malaysia is 'fused'. The Malaysian lawyer may act as both an advocate and a solicitor. Lawyers in Malaysia can practice in the government or private sector. Lawyers in the government sector are administered by the Judicial and Legal Service Commission. There is no division of legal profession in private practice.

The legal profession in Singapore is also 'fused'. A Singaporean lawyer may act as both an advocate and a solicitor. The lawyer may serve in different roles, such as a legal or judicial officer in the Singapore Legal Service, an in-house counsel of a company, or can practice law in a local or international law firm. If the lawyer chooses to work in the local firm, he/she generally handles litigation, corporate work, conveyancing, and intellectual property work. On the other hand, a lawyer in an international law firm is

[6] See http://international.lawsociety.org.uk/ip/asia/1073/practise (last accessed on January 1, 2015).
[7] See http://en.wikipedia.org/wiki/Barrister#Japan (last accessed on January 1, 2015).

generally limited to sophisticated corporate, finance, and banking transactions. The Law Society of Singapore primarily upholds the interests of the practicing lawyers, while the Singapore Academy of Law seeks to advance the legal profession as a whole (Sim 2007).

In the UK, the legal profession is divided into two distinct branches, namely solicitors and barristers. Solicitors undertake most of the work in magistrates' courts and county courts—both preparation of cases and also advocacy. Litigation is only a small part of the work of the solicitor's profession as a whole. Most are involved in commercial work relating to business, e.g., dealing with commercial transactions, corporate matters, land, share, and other property dealings. There is also a large amount of private client work which does not involve any litigation such as the conveyancing of houses, making wills, advising on tax matters, and so on. The traditional work of barristers is advocacy—they present cases in court, where their ability to speak and to think quickly "on their feet" as the evidence unfolds is what they are skilled in. The barrister will be "briefed" (instructed) by a solicitor—it is the solicitor who first contacts the client and has initial conduct of the case. However, the barrister is to a fair extent independent of the solicitor and can take an independent judgment as to how to conduct the case.

Barristers are occasionally advocates in magistrates' courts (more commonly in London than elsewhere), but they mainly work in the Crown Court (it is possible to have a solicitor advocate but this is still rare), the High Court, or in appeal courts. Barristers also deal with advice on litigation and the drafting of documents (pleadings) related to litigation.[8]

The legal profession in the US is unitary, and a US lawyer may act as both an advocate and a solicitor. After passing a Bar examination and after being admitted to practice, all lawyers may prosecute or defend in the courts of the state where they are admitted. Regulation of the US legal profession arises principally

---

[8] See http://ttallislaw.weebly.com/uploads/4/5/7/9/4579552/the_legal_system.pdf (last accessed on January 1, 2015).

under professional rules adopted by state and federal courts, with supervisory oversight delegated largely to State Bar Associations.

A cross comparison of these countries also reveals that separate boards and councils are responsible for different regulatory functions within the sector. For instance, in Malaysia, there is a separate disciplinary board for advocates and solicitors and another separate legal professional qualifying board, indicating that disciplinary issues are separated from education and training responsibilities. In the case of Australia, there are separate sections that have been created within the law council to deal with issues of reforms, international law, and legal practice. A separate Australian Law Reform Commission is also present to help the government take informed decisions on the legal sector. In Singapore, there is the Legal Education Board, the Law Society, the Law Academy, and the Attorney General's Chambers which address different issues within the sector.

Practice Requirements

Practice requirements pertain to the rules laid down by the professional bodies/concerned agencies in the legal sector which enable the law professionals to become members and to get licenses and practice. It is used as an oversight mechanism to ensure professionals self-regulate and follow certain codes of conduct. Though the practice requirements vary across countries, generally, legal professionals are required to be a member of one or more local registration bodies in all countries. The following discussion highlights the requirements for obtaining membership of the professional association/s and outlines some of the concerned regulatory bodies involved in this process in these countries.

Australia follows a two-step process for admission to practice. Graduates must first obtain admission as a lawyer in the state/territory, which requires both possession of a recognized law degree and good character, plus completion of a postgraduate Practical Legal Training (PLT) course. The law degree requires a minimum of four years' coursework, although most students complete a five-year program including study of another discipline (such as business, engineering, or medicine). Completion of the law degree is followed by a period of PLT that may take the form of a practical training course at a law school, an apprenticeship with a legal practitioner (known as "articles of clerkship"), or a combination of the two. There are no mandatory practice requirements for law degrees, although state/territorial licensing bodies uniformly require coursework in civil procedure and ethics, among other subject areas. Licensing requirements are enacted by each state or territory, although the Law Council of Australia's model professional rules have been adopted by nearly every jurisdiction. Lawyers then apply to the applicable state private legal organization for certificates of practice as either solicitors (requiring nothing further, beyond the application) or barristers (requiring a passing score on the State Bar Exam). Although there is a nominal distinction between solicitors and barristers, today the professions are largely fused in Australia (Harvard Law School Program on the Legal Profession 2011a).

Legal practitioners in most jurisdictions across Australia are also required to undertake mandatory continuing professional development (CPD) activity in order to maintain their practicing certificate. The CPD requirements vary for each state and territory in Australia.

To be admitted to practice in China one has to have basic licensing. The PRC nationals (or Hong Kong permanent residents who do not hold a foreign passport) are the only people able to obtain PRC practicing certificates. The first step toward this is to complete an integrated four-year bachelor of law course directly after the secondary school. Thereafter, a person should clear the national judicial examination though graduates holding bachelor's degrees in fields other than law may also sit for the PRC national judicial examination. In addition to an academic degree and passage of the national judicial examination, aspiring lawyers must also complete a one-year internship in a PRC law firm to qualify as a practicing lawyer (Harvard Law School Program on the Legal Profession 2011b).

To practice in Japan, one has to be admitted to the Japanese Federation of Bar Associations (Nichibenren) (JFBA). Qualification for legal practice requires a graduate Juris Doctor (JD) course that lasts two years (for students who have already completed an LLB) or three years (for those with nonlaw undergraduate degrees). The Bar exam is the second step in professional legal training. On an average, 40–50 percent of law school graduates pass the Bar exam (passage numbers are capped by a quota). Special institution run by the Supreme Courts, called the Legal Training and Research Institute, take those clearing the Bar and train them for a one-year period. After such training, a person can be admitted to the Bar. Pursuant to the Lawyers Act, those who pass the Bar exam and participate in the apprenticeship program are eligible to join the Bar Association and become licensed. Continuing education programs for practicing attorneys are conducted both by the JFBA and each Local Bar Association (Harvard Law School Program on the Legal Profession 2011b).

To be admitted to the Malaysian Bar, an aspirant has to first attain the status of a 'qualified person' by obtaining a law degree. One can receive a Bachelor of Laws of the University of Malaya, the University of Malaya in Singapore, the University of Singapore, or the National University of Singapore; a barrister-at-law of England or Ireland; or a law degree from Australia or New Zealand. For the recognition of lawyers holding degrees from Australia and New Zealand, the qualifying board determines the university whose LLB degree is to be recognized and specifies additional requirements to be satisfied before the holder of that LLB degree is deemed to be a qualified person. Second, the aspirant is required to have a certificate of legal practice. A necessary preliminary to obtaining the practicing certificate is the issue of a Sijil Annual from the Bar Council.[9] A 'qualified person' is also required to serve a period of pupillage for a period of nine months (the prescribed period is nine months but the Bar Council may exempt a qualified person from any period up to six months pupillage) (Kuala Lumpur Bar Committee 2011).

There is one Bar for Peninsular Malaysia namely the Bar Council of Malaysia and a separate Bar each for Sabah and Sarawak, the

---

[9] 'Sijil Annual' means the certificate issued by the Bar Council under Section 32 of the Legal Profession Act, 1976, of Malaysia.

Sabah Law Association and the Advocates Association of Sarawak, respectively. A member of the Peninsular Malaysia Bar is not entitled to practice in Sabah and Sarawak. No member of the Bar in Sabah or Sarawak is entitled to practice in the other state or in Peninsular Malaysia. Malaysia introduced a CPD Scheme in 2012. All practicing advocates and solicitors of the Malaysian Bar and pupils in chambers are subject to the CPD scheme.

In Singapore, in order to be admitted to the Singapore Bar, an aspirant has to first attain the status of a 'qualified person' by obtaining a law degree. One can receive a law degree from the National University of Singapore or from one of the approved overseas universities of the UK, the US, Australia, Canada, and New Zealand. The law graduates from the approved foreign universities are also required to complete the Diploma in Singapore Law conferred by the National University of Singapore. Second, one has to clear the Postgraduate Law Course (PLC) exams conducted by the Board of Legal Education. It is a full time course conducted for a period of five months.

Singapore introduced a new system wherein law firms are responsible for providing structured training to fresh graduates for six months. It replaced the existing pupillage system in which a senior lawyer takes care of the graduate for six months. Apart from these requirements, an aspirant is also required to clear specified dining requirements. In 1999, the Board introduced an institution called "Edu-Dine" for PLC students. The primary objective is to provide a congenial forum where, over three dinners, students may interact with judges, senior lawyers, law academics, etc., so as to know them better and to develop a collegiate spirit among members of the legal fraternity (Cheng n.d.).

Like Malaysia, the Compulsory CPD scheme was introduced in Singapore in 2012. As per this scheme, advocates and solicitors admitted to the Singapore Bar on or after January 2, 2007, must meet the CPD requirements set out in the Legal Profession (CPD) Rules 2012.

As mentioned earlier, the UK has a legal profession made up of solicitors and barristers, represented by the Law Society of England

and Wales and the Bar Council, respectively. In order to qualify as a solicitor, one requires a qualifying law degree, completion of a Legal Practice Course (LPC), a training contract, and passing the Professional Skills Course (PSC). The steps typically taken to become a barrister involve three main stages of training—Academic Stage: an undergraduate degree in law (LLB), or an undergraduate degree in any other subject followed by the conversion course; Vocational Stage: the Bar Professional Training Course (BPTC), which entails one year of full time study or two years' part time study; Pupillage: one year spent as a pupil in barristers' chambers or in another organization approved by the Bar Standards Board as a Pupillage Training Organization (PTO). After training, the final stage is to obtain tenancy in a set of barristers' chambers as a self-employed barrister, or to go into practice as an employed barrister.[10]

The UK also mandates Compulsory CPD requirements for both solicitors and barristers. All solicitors and registered European lawyers (RELs) who are in legal practice or employment in England and Wales and work 32 hours or more per week are required to complete a minimum of 16 hours of CPD per year; at least 25 percent of this must consist of participation in accredited training courses.

In the US, students must complete a four-year undergraduate degree in any subject before applying to law school. A three-year JD is usually completed immediately or shortly after completion of the undergraduate degree. Admission into the legal profession begins with pre-legal college education, selective admission to law school, completion of a law degree from an approved law school, passing a rigorous set of written Bar examinations, and meeting a "character and fitness" qualification.

To practice law in the US, a person must be licensed by the state (or admitted to its Bar) under rules established by the state's highest court. All states require a written Bar examination, and most also require a separate written ethics examination. Federal courts and agencies set their own qualifications for those practicing before them,

---

[10] See http://www.barcouncil.org.uk/becoming-a-barrister/how-to-become-a-barrister/ (last accessed on January 1, 2015).

typically accepting lawyers licensed in the state where the court sits. Continuing legal education (CLE) is required in most states of the US. It implies that to maintain a law license lawyers must each year attend legal education courses and seminars, and earn a specified number of educational credits.

Mode of Practice

Lawyers are allowed to practice either as sole proprietorship or as a partnership firm in most of the countries. A few countries also allow the limited liability partnership (LLP) model subject to certain conditions. The following discussion highlights modes of practice for legal professionals and the associated conditions in the selected set of countries.

In Australia, lawyers may practice in sole proprietorships, in general partnerships, in LLPs, and in limited law corporations. With the introduction of the Legal Profession Act (LPA) 2007, solicitors have much more flexibility as to the business structure of their practice. For sole proprietors, a lawyer must hold a principal practicing certificate and for general partnerships, all partners must hold a principal practicing certificate. Lawyers can also form limited law corporations. However, such a corporation must have at least one legal practitioner director (director of company who is the holder of a principal practicing certificate). If they wish to form an LLP or an MDP, they must have at least one legal practitioner partner, who holds a principal practicing certificate, and at least one nonlawyer partner.[11]

China allows solo practitioners, general partnership, special general partnership, and LLPs. Under PRC law, a general partnership law firm (in which each partner shall bear unlimited joint and severable liabilities for the firm's debts) shall have at least three partners. But a special general partnership law firm (in which only one or

---

[11] See www.qls.com.au/files/...6263.../qls_factsheet_-_practice_structures.pdf (last accessed on January 1, 2015).

a few specified partners shall bear unlimited joint and severable liabilities for the firm's debts) shall have at least 20 partners. LLP is permitted but if Chinese lawyers choose to practice with a foreign law firm (FLF) their license will be cancelled (Harvard Law School Program on the Legal Profession 2011b).

In Malaysia, lawyers may practice in sole proprietorships and in general partnerships. LLPs are, however, allowed now with the passage of the LLP Act in 2011, though there is need for clarity on various provisions of the Act in the context of the legal services sector.

In Japan, lawyers may practice in sole proprietorships, in general partnerships, in legal professional corporations, and in joint enterprises. Though, the most dominant firm structure is sole proprietorships or small partnerships, joint enterprises are the most common structure chosen by foreign firms. The LLP Act is in force since August 2005 but in the case of Malaysia, there is a need for clarity on various issues in the context of this sector.

Singapore allows lawyers to practice in sole proprietorships, general partnerships, LLPs, and law corporations. Solicitors may also practice on a temporary or freelance basis as a locum solicitor. Small law firms are also allowed to form a group law practice. Large firms having specialization in corporate and banking and finance are allowed to practice jointly with international law firms through joint law ventures (JLVs) and formal law alliances (FLAs). Lawyers admitted on or after March 1, 1997, cannot practice as a sole proprietor or partner for the first three years of practice. After three years of practice, lawyers are allowed to practice without any restriction as a partner or director. However, a lawyer is required to complete the Law Society's Legal Practice Management Course in order to practice as a sole proprietor, even after three years of practice. The minister for law may exempt a solicitor from this restriction after satisfying that the solicitor has gained substantial experience in law in Singapore or elsewhere. A solicitor may be exempted from this restriction. Singapore passed the LLPs Act in 2005. Limited Law Corporations are also allowed with the enactment of the Legal Profession (Amendment) Act 2000 (Cheng n.d.).

In the UK (England and Wales), there are three main types of firms that are authorized to operate, namely, recognized bodies, recognized sole practitioners, and licensed bodies. Recognized bodies are firms where all the managers (i.e., members in an LLP, partners in a partnership, and directors in a company) and interest holders are lawyers. On the other hand, licensed bodies are firms where there is a nonlawyer interest of at least 10 percent in a firm, such as, a manager who is a nonlawyer or an external investor who is a nonlawyer.

In order to become a recognized sole practitioner, one needs to apply to the Solicitors Regulation Authority (SRA) and receive authorization from the SRA before commencing the practice. It is to be noted that if the practice is setup with a salaried partner, then the person is not authorized to practice as a sole practitioner. Salaried partners are treated as full partners for the purpose of authorization and as such practice is authorized as a recognized partnership.

The UK also allows alternative business structures (ABSs) that allow solicitors and other approved persons to enter business with nonlawyers, as long as at least one of the managers of that business is a solicitor, an REL, or a person authorized by another approved regulator. There are no restrictions on the structure of a licensed body and there is no service requirement.[12]

In the US, the allowed modes of practice vary from states to state. For instance, in the Florida Bar, lawyers may practice law in the form of professional service corporations, professional limited liability companies, sole proprietorships, general partnerships, or LLPs organized or qualified under applicable law. In the New York City Bar, one can practice as a sole proprietor, a single member professional service limited liability company (LLC or PLLC); a single member professional service corporation (PC); as partners; a professional limited liability partnership (LLP or PLLP); a professional limited liability company (LLC or PLLC); or a professional service corporation (PC).[13]

---

[12] See http://www.lawsociety.org.uk/advice/practice-notes/setting-up-a-practice-regulatory-requirements/ (last accessed on January 1, 2015).

[13] See http://www.nycbar.org/small-law-firm-center/slf-resources/767-slf-faqs (last accessed on January 1, 2015).

Regulations on Advertising

Countries have varying regulations on advertising and soliciting of business by legal professionals. This is because of differences in the scope of practice across countries as well as differences in the ideological approach to this profession, with some countries seeing this as a profession and others viewing it also as a business.

The law Council in Australia permits advertising, and lawyers are required to follow the regulations adopted under the Australian Solicitors Conduct Rules 2011. According to these rules, a solicitor must not convey a false, misleading, or deceptive impression of specialist expertise, and must not advertise or authorize advertising in a manner that uses the words "accredited specialist" or a derivative of those words (including post-nominals), unless the solicitor is a specialist accredited by the relevant professional body.[14]

China also has specific rules in relation to advertising. These rules are passed by the All China Lawyers Association to govern advertising and practicing activities of lawyers. These rules include specific provisions on the use of names by lawyers or law firms.

In Japan, though advertising has been liberalized in principle, it is still subject to many restrictions. Malaysia allows a very limited form of advertisement. Legal firms in Malaysia can provide free legal education and advice in newspaper columns with the aim of building up a client-based relationship and raising public awareness.

In Singapore, publicity in some forms of advertisement is permitted. However, publicity as an advocate and solicitor or law practice must not be false, misleading, deceptive, inaccurate, or unbefitting the dignity of the legal profession. Special attention is required to be paid before making a claim to any expertise or specialization in any field of law. Title descriptions of lawyers require the Council's approval and any descriptions not expressly permitted by the Council may only be used with the Council's prior written approval. Apart from these, Singapore also specifies the rules for the use of corporate stationary, visiting cards, and computer software. The Law Society (Publicity) Rules set out what

[14] See www.lawcouncil.asn.au/ (last accessed on January 1, 2015).

can be contained in any marketing material connected with law practice. However, such restrictions do not apply if the publicity is intended for use outside Singapore.[15]

Publicity through most mediums of advertisement is permitted in the UK. However, publicity in relation to the concerned law firm or in-house practice or for any other business must be accurate and not misleading. It should not diminish the trust the public places in the provision of legal services. It is also required to ensure that one does not make unsolicited approaches in person or by telephone to members of the public in order to publicize one's firm or in-house practice or another business. The publicity material should contain appropriate information so that the clients and the public have sufficient information about the legal practitioner, the firm, and how it is being regulated. The letterhead, web site, and e-mails should show the words "authorized and regulated by the Solicitors Regulation Authority" and either the firm's registered name and number (if it is an LLP or company) or if the firm is a partnership or sole practitioner, the name under which it is licensed/authorized by the SRA and the number allocated to it by the SRA.[16]

In the US, individual Bar associations continue to restrict and regulate advertisements. The American Bar Association (ABA) as a whole has also laid down a legal standard that regulates advertising. According to the ABA rules, a lawyer may advertise services through written, recorded, or electronic communication, including public media. However, a lawyer shall not give anything of value to a person for recommending the lawyer's services except that a lawyer may pay the reasonable costs of advertisements or communications permitted by this rule and pay the usual charges of a legal service plan or a not-for-profit or qualified lawyer referral service. A lawyer may refer clients to another lawyer or a nonlawyer professional pursuant to an agreement not otherwise prohibited.

[15] See http://www.lawsociety.org.sg/forMembers/ResourceCentre/Running YourPractice/StartingaPractice/AGuidetoStartingaPractice/WhatEveryLawyer-ShouldKnow.aspx#14 (last accessed on January 1, 2015).

[16] See http://www.sra.org.uk/solicitors/handbook/code/content.page (last accessed on January 1, 2015).

As far as the communication of fields of practice and specialization is concerned, a lawyer may communicate the fact that the lawyer does or does not practice in particular fields of law. A lawyer shall not state or imply that he/she is certified as a specialist in a particular field of law, unless the lawyer has been certified as a specialist by an organization that has been approved by an appropriate state authority or that has been accredited by the ABA; and the name of the certifying organization is clearly identified in the communication.[17]

Indemnity Insurance Requirements

Law practices and Australian-registered foreign lawyers engaged in legal practice are required to hold professional indemnity insurance in some of the states. The Legal Services Board may grant an exemption to a law practice or community legal center from the requirement to obtain or maintain professional indemnity insurance. In China and Japan, indemnity insurance is not mandatory. In Malaysia, every practicing member of the Bar must be covered by professional indemnity against professional liability. In Singapore, all practicing lawyers are required to maintain a minimum amount of professional indemnity insurance against loss arising from professional negligence and other claims. The minimum coverage for each claim is US$1 million for sole proprietorships and general partnerships and US$2 million for LLCs and LLPs.[18]

In the UK, professional indemnity insurance is required by solicitors' firms and is administered by the SRA. In the US, Oregon is currently the only state that requires lawyers to carry liability insurance. Though it is not mandatory, seven states currently require lawyers to disclose their professional liability insurance status

---

[17] See http://www.americanbar.org/groups/professional_responsibility/publications/model_rules_of_professional_conduct/rule_7_2_advertising.html (last accessed on January 1, 2015).

[18] See http://www.lawsociety.org.sg/forMembers/ResourceCentre/Running YourPractice/StartingaPractice/AGuidetoStartingaPractice/WhatEveryLawyer-ShouldKnow.aspx#7 (last accessed on January 1, 2015).

directly to clients, according to the ABA Standing Committee on Client Protection. Eighteen other states have implemented rules requiring disclosure of such insurance status as part of the lawyer's annual Bar registration, rather than disclosing directly to clients.[19]

Entry Regulations for Foreign Legal Professionals

Countries have different regulations for legal practice in their countries by foreign professionals. They prescribe entry norms with respect to training and qualifications, registration requirements, membership with the local body, residency, and immigration requirements which can affect the ability of foreign legal professionals to access their markets and the scope of their practice. The following discussion highlights the main regulatory requirements imposed on foreign legal professionals seeking to enter in these countries for providing legal services.

A foreign lawyer can practice foreign law in Australia. Foreign legal practice shall be subject to all applicable state laws governing the legal profession and under the control of the state law society in whose state the foreign lawyer wishes to practice. The right to practice or advise on domestic law is reserved for domestic lawyers by the state governing the legal profession. A foreign lawyer is prohibited from practicing law or holding himself out as qualified to practice law in Australia until he is accredited as a foreign lawyer. An accredited foreign lawyer shall not carry on foreign legal practice under the name of any FLF unless it is a recognized FLF. A FLF shall be prohibited from establishing an office and carrying on business in Australia until it is recognized as a FLF. Upon recognition as a FLF, those partners in the FLF who have become or will become accredited foreign lawyers may carry on their foreign legal practice, from the date of their respective accreditation, as principals in the relevant state.

---

[19] See http://apps.americanbar.org/litigation/litigationnews/top_stories/professional-liability-insurance-states.html (last accessed on January 1, 2015).

Full service legal practice could be done in collaboration with domestic lawyers. Application may be made to a state law society by a domestic lawyer or by a domestic law firm for approval to practice as an integrated legal practice under the same name as a recognized FLF and to share the receipts of that practice with the partners of the recognized FLF.

A foreign lawyer in Australia may with or without accreditation be employed at any time by a domestic lawyer. A foreign lawyer (whether accredited or not) may be employed by a domestic lawyer, or may be engaged by a domestic lawyer as a consultant on foreign law, so long as the foreign lawyer does not act as a domestic lawyer (Law Council of Australia n.d.).

In China, FLFs are subject to a number of barriers. These barriers primarily apply to commercial work, whether of a consultancy or litigation nature. Chinese lawyers have been subject to considerable political pressures for the type of work that they perform. FLFs do little, if any, work involving advice on Chinese criminal law.

It is generally observed that international law firms are unable to hire or be owned by qualified PRC lawyers with active PRC law licenses in China. This is due to the fact that under current legal regulations, a licensed PRC lawyer must first suspend his or her license and may not practice PRC law while at an international law firm in China. Foreign lawyers cannot sit for the Bar exam or practice Chinese law. Foreign lawyers are restricted in their appearances before PRC government agencies. Although China was required to permit foreign lawyers "to provide information on the impact of the Chinese legal environment" as part of its WTO accession, foreign lawyers are frequently barred from participating in certain types of meetings with Chinese government agencies, even when in the company of local counsel.

FLFs also experience burdensome representative office registration requirements in China. FLFs must justify the need to establish their representative office by the "social and economic development conditions of the proposed location" and other vague considerations. A FLF must also wait three years after opening its first representative office before it can open another. FLFs also face discriminatory tax treatment as FLFs potentially face double taxation on profits while a domestic firm only experiences one level of taxation at a lower rate (Cohen 2012).

In Malaysia, FLFs are allowed to operate either as an international partnership with a Malaysian law firm or as a qualified foreign law firm (QFLF). Alternatively, a Malaysian law firm may choose to employ a foreign lawyer. An international partnership is defined as a partnership between a FLF and a Malaysian law firm, while a QFLF is a stand-alone foreign firm which does not require a Malaysian law firm as a partner. Licenses for international partnerships and QFLFs will be for a period of three years and are renewable. A Malaysian law firm will be granted a three-year license to employ a foreign lawyer. It is to be noted that all individual foreign lawyers working in international partnerships, QFLFs or Malaysian law firms are required to be registered as foreign lawyers. Registrations may be granted subject to terms and conditions and will have to be renewed annually.

International partnerships, QFLFs, and individual foreign lawyers employed by Malaysian law firms are, however, allowed to practice only in the permitted practice areas. Practice in the permitted practice areas specifically exclude: constitutional and administrative law, conveyancing; criminal law; family law; succession law, including wills, intestate succession, probate and administration; trust law, where the settlor is an individual, and the law relating to charities and trust foundations, whether the settlor is an individual or a corporation; retail banking, including corporate or commercial loans to SMEs; registration of intellectual property; appearing or pleading in any court of justice in Malaysia, representing a client in any proceedings instituted in such a court or giving advice, whether or not the main purpose of which is to advise the client on the conduct of such proceedings (with certain exceptions); and appearing in any hearing before a quasi-judicial or regulatory body, authority or tribunal in Malaysia (with certain exceptions).

Malaysia also allows foreign lawyers advising on non-Malaysian law to come to Malaysia and work on a project for up to 60 days in a calendar year, subject to immigration approval. Foreign lawyers are also allowed to enter Malaysia for arbitral proceedings (The Malaysian Bar Press Release 2014).

A foreign lawyer can practice foreign law in Japan. The system of gaikokuho-jimu-bengoshi (GJB) was introduced by the act on special measures concerning the handling of legal services by foreign lawyers. A GJB, a registered foreign lawyer, is a person whose professional duties are providing legal services in a foreign jurisdiction, with a qualification equivalent to the Japanese attorney qualification (a qualification to be a foreign lawyer) and who has obtained approval of the minister of justice and registered in the roll of registered foreign lawyers kept by the JFBA.

The revised GJB Act (enforced on April 1, 2005) lifted the prohibitions on employment of attorneys by GJBs, joint enterprises, and profit distributions. The revised GJB Act requires GJBs who are to employ or engage in joint enterprises with Japanese attorneys to notify the JFBA. Furthermore, in order to prevent GJBs from engaging in conduct beyond the scope of permitted practices, the law puts a certain restriction on the conduct of GJBs and employed attorneys.

Japan also adopts the limited licensing system. This means that foreign lawyers are not required to clear an exam but they have to satisfy a three-year practice experience requirement in their home country among other minor requirements. Registered foreign lawyers (i.e., a GJB) are permitted to employ Japanese-qualified lawyers (bengoshi). However, a registered lawyer (GJB) cannot practice Japanese law and their scope of practice is generally limited to practicing the law of their home country.

Registered foreign lawyers/foreign firms are allowed to freely carry on the business of a legal practice with bengoshi. This can be either by admitting bengoshi as partners or entering into some other form of business collaboration, such as a joint venture (JV). However there is a requirement for the bengoshi to have at least five years of work experience. Registered foreign lawyers/foreign firms may also establish legal professional corporations through which they can carry on their legal practice in Japan.[20]

[20] See http://www.lawcouncil.asn.au/lawcouncil/images/LCA-PDF/Country_Fact_Sheets/Japan.pdf (last accessed on January 1, 2015).

A foreign lawyer can practice foreign law in Singapore, including his or her home country law, a third-country law, or international law without re-qualifying. They are regulated by the Legal Profession (International Services) Secretariat of the Attorney-General's Chambers. Foreign lawyers are prohibited from practicing Singapore law. A FLF cannot employ a Singapore qualified lawyer to practice Singapore law or hold shares of any kind in a Singapore law firm. Foreign lawyers are free to constitute an LLP to practice foreign law subject to the written approval of the Attorney-General's office. FLFs can only provide legal services in relation to Singapore law through a JLV or FLA with a Singapore law firm. This is subject to a series of conditions and requirements.[21]

In the UK, partnerships with English solicitors are possible only if the foreign lawyer registers with the Law Society as a registered foreign lawyer. They are then subject to some restrictions. For market access of natural persons in the UK, a lawyer is required to have a university degree, professional qualifications, and three years of professional experience in the sector.

Foreign lawyers do not have the rights of audience in the courts. Certain practices are limited to nationals like conducting litigation, drawing up court documents, property transfer and succession and immigration advice and immigration services. Immigration barriers are also in place in the UK. A letter of no-objection is required from the Law Society and evidence of financial standing should be provided in order to get a work visa. Professional indemnity insurance is also mandatory.

In the US, according to the ABA, only five states will allow a foreign lawyer to take the Bar under any circumstances: New York, California, Alabama, New Hampshire, and Virginia. Depending on the lawyer's practice, this may limit the locations where he or she can practice. There are different restrictions in various states on work permits. Foreign attorney are subject to different visa regulations to work in different states in the US.

---

[21] See http://www.legalservices.apec.org/inventory/singapore.html (last accessed on January 1, 2015).

FDI Regulations for Foreign Law Firms

A comparison of FDI regulations across some selected countries reveals that most of these countries allow FDI in legal services, either partially or fully, though there are associated conditions on such FDI. For instance, according to the Legal Profession (Licensing of International Partnerships and Qualified FLFs and Registration of Foreign Lawyers) Rules 2014 of Malaysia, the equity ownership and voting rights of the Malaysian law firm and the FLF in the international partnership are to be determined by the selection committee based on the business plan submitted as part of the application process. The Malaysian Bar recommends that the Malaysian law firm should not have less than 60 percent and the FLF should not have more than 40 percent of the equity and voting rights and of the total number of lawyers in the international partnership.[22]

In Singapore, according to the Legal Profession (Amendment) Act 2012, foreign law practice, with the approval of the Attorney-General, can be a shareholder in any Singaporean law practice which is a law corporation and can share the profits of any Singapore law practice. In Australia, the acquisition of substantial interests by foreigners must be notified to the respective state legal council. The UK also allows FDI in legal services. In the US, FDI in legal services is permitted in some states. However, the restrictions vary from state to state.

The above discussion on various regulations prevailing in the selected set of countries reveals that these countries differ in their regulatory setup for legal services. The nature of regulations depends on the market structure, i.e., how fragmented is the market, the degree of specialization, whether the sector is seen as a profession or as a business, and the nature of training, among other factors. Licensing norms and registration requirements are the

---

[22] See http://www.malaysianbar.org.my/trade_in_legal_services_formerly_known_as_gats/liberalisation_of_legal_services.html (last accessed on January 1, 2015).

main constraint to the operation of foreign firms and professionals while regulations on advertising are the main domestic regulatory constraint. It is worth noting that most of these countries started reforming this sector internally as well as for foreign law practitioners, as reflected in the amendment of rules in the legal profession in these countries over the years.

OECD Cross-country Indicators of Restrictiveness for Legal Services[23]

Several multilateral agencies have in recent years attempted to quantify the incidence of regulatory barriers and their trends over time for selected countries, across a range of services, including legal services. One of such restrictiveness indicators is that prepared by the OECD based on product market regulations for nonmanufacturing sectors. For these indicators, legal services are included within the broad category of professional services, and the indicators are calculated for a selected set of countries for the years 1996, 2003, 2008, and 2013. These indicators capture the domestic regulatory conditions across various dimensions including regulatory requirements and restrictions faced by foreign legal professionals in terms of accessing these markets as well as in operating in these markets once they have entered. In accordance with this, the regulations included for constructing the indicators consist of 'entry regulations' and 'conduct regulations'. Entry regulations mainly include barriers to becoming a member of the profession. These may exist in the form of licensing and educational requirements, quantitative constraints on the number of suppliers of professional services and/or exclusive rights granted to suppliers in certain areas. On the other hand, conduct regulations include

---

[23] Based on OECD Database on Professional Services Indicators available at http://www.oecd.org/economy/growth/indicatorsofproductmarketregulation-homepage.htm#indicators (last accessed on January 1, 2015).

restrictions on prices and fees, advertising, form of business, and inter-professional cooperation. Thus, the indicators cover restrictions that are imposed either by law or by self-regulatory arrangements of the profession.

The indicator is calculated as the simple average of the indicators of entry and conduct regulation. Table A.3 shows the coding and weights for the various entry regulations and conduct-related measures. An index value of 0 represents 'least restrictive', while an index value of 6 stands for 'most restrictive'. The indicators of regulation in professional services suggest that, on average across the OECD countries, legal services is the profession in which most regulatory hurdles are found.

A graphical representation of the OECD indicators for selected countries is presented in Figure 3.1 and Table 3.1. Although the OECD database covers a wide range of countries, only those countries that are common to the ones discussed earlier in this chapter, namely, Australia, Japan, the UK, and the US, are mentioned here. China and Malaysia could not be covered for this purpose as their indicators are not available from the OECD database.[24]

The trends in the OECD indicators show that the four developed countries in this sample have undergone liberalization in this sector

Figure 3.1
Trends in OECD Indicators for Legal Services for Selected Countries

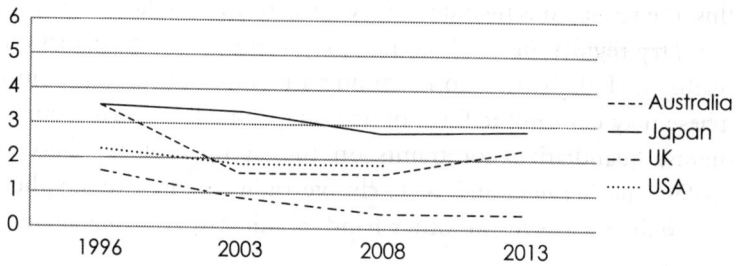

Source: OECD Indicators of Product Market Regulation.

[24] For further details on the methodology, see Conway and Nicoletti (2006).

Table 3.1
OECD Indicators for Legal Services, Selected Years

	Legal Services Indicators			
Country	1996	2003	2008	2013
Australia	3.46	1.58	1.58	2.31
Japan	3.50	3.38	2.75	2.83
UK	1.63	0.85	0.42	0.42
USA	2.25	1.81	1.81	

Source: OECD Indicators of Product Market Regulation.

over the 1996–2013 period. While the UK was the most open country for legal services in 2013, Japan was the most restrictive country amongst the selected set of countries.

A detailed analysis of the entry and conduct regulations, as reflected in Table 3.2 (a and b), shows the most restrictive elements of regulation for these countries. For Australia, exclusive or shared exclusive rights, education requirements, and advertising regulations contribute most to the indicator value. For Japan, exclusive or shared exclusive rights, compulsory chamber membership, advertising regulations, and inter-professional cooperation are important regulatory elements. The UK is the most liberal legal services market and the only significant regulation is advertising. The US has education requirements, quotas and economic needs test, and advertising as the most significant entry and conduct regulations.

Overall, the above illustration of regulatory measures and the variety in the nature and content of these measures across countries indicates the jurisdiction-specific issues in any analysis of the legal services sector. It is evident from the above discussion that any discussions on deregulating and liberalizing legal services are bound to be shaped by the prevailing regulatory environment and will need to take into account the varying regulatory characteristics and concerns across countries.

Table 3.2
OECD Indicators for Entry and Conduct Regulations for Legal Services, Selected Years

a. Entry Regulations

Country	Entry Regulations				Exclusive or Shared Exclusive Rights				Education Requirements				Compulsory Chamber Membership				Quotas and Economic Needs Tests			
	1996	2003	2008	2013	1996	2003	2008	2013	1996	2003	2008	2013	1996	2003	2008	2013	1996	2003	2008	2013
Australia	4.42	2.42	2.42	3.88	6.00	6.00	6.00	6.00	5.67	3.67	3.67	3.50	0.00	0.00	0.00	6.00	6.00	0.00	0.00	0.00
Japan	3.50	3.50	3.50	3.67	6.00	6.00	6.00	6.00	2.00	2.00	2.00	2.67	6.00	6.00	6.00	6.00	0.00	0.00	0.00	0.00
UK	2.50	0.96	0.08	0.08	6.00	0.00	0.00	0.00	4.00	3.83	0.33	0.33	0.00	0.00	0.00	0.00	0.00	0.00	0.00	0.00
USA	4.00	2.88	2.88	–	6.00	1.50	1.50	–	4.00	4.00	4.00	–	0.00	0.00	0.00	–	6.00	6.00	6.00	–

b. Conduct Regulations

Country	Conduct Regulations				Regulations on Prices and Fees				Regulations on Advertising				Regulations on the Form of Business				Inter-professional Cooperation			
	1996	2003	2008	2013	1996	2003	2008	2013	1996	2003	2008	2013	1996	2003	2008	2013	1996	2003	2008	2013
Australia	2.50	0.75	0.75	0.75	5.00	0.00	0.00	0.00	3.00	3.00	3.00	3.00	2.00	0.00	0.00	0.00	0.00	0.00	0.00	0.00
Japan	3.50	3.25	2.00	2.00	2.00	5.00	0.00	0.00	3.00	3.00	3.00	3.00	6.00	2.00	2.00	2.00	3.00	3.00	3.00	3.00
UK	0.75	0.75	0.75	0.75	0.00	0.00	0.00	0.00	3.00	3.00	3.00	3.00	0.00	0.00	0.00	0.00	0.00	0.00	0.00	0.00
USA	0.50	0.75	0.75	–	0.00	0.00	0.00	–	0.00	3.00	3.00	–	2.00	0.00	0.00	–	0.00	0.00	0.00	–

Source: OECD Indicators of Product Market Regulation.

4

Legal Services in India

India has the second largest number of lawyers in the world, second only to the US. The number of lawyers in India is estimated at approximately one million, and the number of law colleges in India is around 900 spread across the country. These Indian law schools graduate thousands of lawyers each year.[1] Most of these lawyers represent clients in courts and other judicial bodies, working as solo practitioners or in family-run concerns.

The Indian law firms are mostly of small size with less than five partners. Only a handful of law firms in India have 20 partners, which is the maximum number of partners permitted per firm under of the 1956 Companies Act of India.[2] Since the 1990s, there has also been a rapid growth in a new breed of Indian corporate lawyers who serve the expanding commercial sector, both domestic and international. They comprise over 150 larger law firms (the five largest of which now have more than 200 lawyers each) operating mostly from the major business centers in India, i.e., Mumbai, Delhi, and Bangalore. They provide advice on transactions and other related services to Indian and multinational corporate clients.

---

[1] See http://outsourceportfolio.com/lpo-career-lawyers-law-graduates/ and http://www.barcouncilofindia.org/about/about-the-legal-profession/ (both accessed on January 1, 2015).

[2] According to Section 4 of the Companies Act, 1956, the number of partners in a firm shall not exceed 20, and a partnership having more than 20 persons would be considered as illegal. The Companies Act, 2013 eliminated this restriction.

There is also an expanding 'in-house counsel' sector, comprising of Indian lawyers working in the legal departments of domestic and foreign companies.

According to the Economic Survey, 2012–2013, legal services in India grew at a steady rate of 8.2 percent between 2005–2006 and 2011–2012. Over the years, legal professionals in India have developed expertise in new and emerging areas of practice, such as mergers and acquisitions, infrastructure financing, public–private partnerships (PPPs), etc. Many of the qualified Indian lawyers from the esteemed law schools in India are in great demand in other countries, such as the UK and the US.

Historical Evolution[3]

The roots of legal profession in India lie in its enriched ancient civilization. From being religiously prescribed to the current constitutional and legal systems, the legal profession in India has traversed through secular legal systems and the system of common law. In ancient India, secular law was practiced and varied in form and content from region to region and from ruler to ruler. Many ruling dynasties of ancient India had court systems for civil and criminal matters. For instance, the Mauryas (321–185 BC) and the Mughals (16th–19th centuries) had excellent secular court systems. The Mughal legal system gave way to the current common law system.

The common law system came to India with the British East India Company which was granted charter by King George I in 1726 to establish "Mayor's Courts" in Madras, Bombay, and Calcutta. After the First War of Independence in 1857, the control of company territories in India passed to the British Crown which led to significant changes in the Indian legal system. For instance, the

---

[3] Based on information available at BCI web site http://www.barcouncilofindia. org/about/about-the-legal-profession/legal-education-in-the-united-kingdom/ (last accessed on January 1, 2015).

Supreme Courts were established replacing the existing mayoral courts. These courts were converted into the High Courts through letters of patents authorized by the Indian High Courts Act passed by the British Parliament in 1862. The right of audience in the newly created Supreme Courts was barred to Indian practitioners and was limited to members of English, Irish, and Scottish professional bodies. The Legal Practitioners Act of 1846 opened up the profession, regardless of nationality or religion.

The Indian Bar Councils Act, 1926, was passed to unify the various grades of legal practice and to provide self-government to the Bars attached to various Courts. The Act required that each High Court must constitute a Bar Council. The duties of the Bar Council were to decide all matters concerning legal education, qualification for enrolment, discipline, and control of the profession. It gave the advocates the authority, previously held by the judiciary, to regulate the membership and discipline their profession. After independence, the Advocates Act, 1961, was passed to give more power and accountability to the profession. This Act gave the Bar Council of India (BCI) the powers to frame rules related to the admission, practice, ethics, privileges, regulations, discipline, and improvement of the profession as well as legal reforms.

Thus, from an artifice of the colonial masters, the Indian legal system has evolved as an essential ingredient of Indian economy and democracy. Today, the legal profession in India is evolving further, entering into new and emerging areas of practice, and is widely viewed as having the potential to become more competitive internationally.

Present Regulatory Framework

Legal services in India are regulated by the BCI under the Advocates Act, 1961, and the BCI Rules, 1975. The Bar Council was constituted under the Advocates Act and it serves as the final regulating body for this sector in India. According to the Advocates Act and the BCI Rules, legal services can be provided only by natural persons who are citizens of India and who are on the rolls of the advocates in states where service is being provided. The service provider can either be a sole proprietorship or a partnership firm consisting of persons similarly qualified to practice law. Thus, apart from the Advocates Act and the BCI Rules, law firms in India are also governed by the Partnership Act, 1932, and to some extent earlier by the Companies Act, 1956 and now by the Companies Act, 2013. Of late, the Government of India has enacted the LLP Act, 2008, which also has a bearing on the formation and working of law firms in India.

The Partnership Act, 1932

The Indian Partnership Act was enacted by the Parliament of India to regulate partnership firms in India in 1932. Before the enactment of this act, partnerships were governed by the provisions of the Indian Contract Act. The Ministry of Corporate Affairs is the nodal ministry to administer this Act. According to this Act, 'partnership' is the relation between persons who have agreed to share the profits of a business carried on by all or any of them acting for all. Persons who have entered into partnership with one another are called individually 'partners' and collectively 'a firm', and the name under which their business is carried on is called the 'firm-name'. It is to be noted that where no provision is made by contract between the partners for the duration of their partnership, or for the determination of their partnership, the partnership is 'partnership-at-will'.

An important feature of this Act relates to the liabilities of a partner in a partnership firm. According to it, every partner is liable, jointly with all the other partners and also severally, for all acts of the firm done while he is a partner. However, the Act is not applicable to the LLPs, as they are governed by the LLP Act, 2008.

It is also to be noted that the Partnership Act defines only the minimum number of partners in a partnership (minimum two partners). It does not put any restrictions on the maximum number of partners in such a partnership. However, the Companies Act, 1956, specified that the maximum number of partners cannot exceed 10 in the case of the banking business and 20 in the case of other business. If the number of partners exceeds the prescribed number, the partnership would be considered as illegal. Thus, according to the provisions of the Partnership Act, 1932, and the Companies Act, 1956, the law firms in India could not have more than 20 partners in a single partnership firm. However, the Companies Act, 2013 eliminated the restriction on the maximum number of partners permitted in a partnership formed by professionals governed by special Acts. Further, this restriction does not apply to the LLPs.

The Limited Liability Partnership Act, 2008

The Parliament of India has enacted the LLP Act, 2008, in January 2009, and it came into effect from April 1, 2009. The LLP Act provides for the formation and regulation of LLPs and matters connected therewith and incidental thereto. According to this Act, the LLP will be a body corporate and a legal entity separate from its partners and it will have a perpetual succession. As mentioned previously, the provisions of the Indian Partnership Act, 1932, will not be applicable to the LLPs.

The Act clearly states that the liability of the partners would be limited to their agreed contribution in the LLP. It also prescribes that no partner would be liable on account of the independent or unauthorized actions of other partners. The partners have the right to manage the business directly and their rights and duties are governed by the agreement between partners. Every partner of an LLP acts as the agent of the LLP but not of other partners whereas in a partnership firm, a partner acts as an agent of other partners. Thus, the Act gives an Indian LLP the same status as of a company in respect of the extent of personal liability of its partners.

An LLP is required to have at least two designated partners who are individuals and at least one of them shall be a resident in India.[4] In the case of LLPs in which all the partners are bodies corporate or in which one or more partners are individuals and body corporate, at least two individuals who are partners of such

---

[4] The term "resident in India" means a person who has stayed in India for a period of not less than 182 days during the immediately preceding one year.

LLPs or nominees of such bodies corporate are required to act as designated partners. Thus, an LLP is required to have a minimum of two partners but there is no limit on the maximum number of partners in such an LLP.

The Bar Council of India[5]

The BCI is a statutory body created by the Parliament of India under the Advocates Act, 1961. It regulates the legal profession in India and also represents the Indian Bar. It performs the regulatory function not only by prescribing standards of professional conduct and etiquette and by exercising disciplinary jurisdiction over the Bar but also by setting standards for legal education. It grants recognition to law colleges and universities for offering law courses which serve as qualification for enrolment as an advocate.

The BCI is statutorily mandated to lay down standards of professional conduct and etiquette for advocates; to safeguard the rights, privileges and interests of advocates; to promote and support law reform; to promote legal education and to lay down standards of legal education; to recognize universities whose degree in law shall be a qualification for enrolment as an advocate; to recognize on a reciprocal basis, the foreign qualifications in law obtained outside India for the purpose of admission as an advocate in India; and to provide for the election of its members who shall run the Bar Councils; among others.

The Advocates Act, 1961[6]

The Advocates Act, 1961, is an Act to amend and consolidate the law relating to legal practitioners and to provide for the constitution of the Bar Councils and an All-India Bar. It lays down various conditions and requirements for practicing law in India, such as

---

[5] Based on information available at the BCI web site http://www.barcouncilofindia.org/about/about-the-bar-council-of-india/ (last accessed on January 1, 2015).

[6] Information in this section is based on the Advocates Act 1961, available at http://www.barcouncilofindia.org/wp-content/uploads/2010/05/Advocates-Act1961.pdf (last accessed on January 1, 2015).

setting up the BCI, State Bar Councils, admission and enrolment of advocates, right to practice, etc.

The Advocates Act requires the establishment of a Bar Council for the territories to which the act extends, to be known as the BCI consisting of attorney-general of India (ex officio member); solicitor-general of India (ex officio member); and one member elected by each State Bar Council from amongst its members. It is to be noted that while some states had a Bar Council of their respective states, some other states have a joint Bar Council. For instance, the states of Andhra Pradesh, Bihar, Gujarat, Jammu and Kashmir, Jharkhand, Madhya Pradesh, Chhattisgarh, Karnataka, Orissa, Rajasthan, Uttar Pradesh, and Uttarakhand have their respective State Bar Councils while for the States of Arunachal Pradesh, Assam, Manipur, Meghalaya, Mizoram, Nagaland, and Tripura, there is to be a State Bar Council, to be known as the Bar Council of Assam, Nagaland, Meghalaya, Manipur, Tripura, Mizoram, and Arunachal Pradesh.

There are two classes of advocates, namely, senior advocates and other advocates. An advocate may, with his consent, be designated as senior advocate if the Supreme Court or a High Court is of opinion that by virtue of his ability (standing at the Bar or special knowledge or experience in law) he is deserving of such distinction. Each State Bar Council is required to prepare and maintain a roll of advocates having names and addresses of persons who are admitted to be advocates on the roll of the State Bar Council.

A person can be admitted as an advocate on a state roll, if he is a citizen of India; completed the age of 21 years; has obtained a degree in law from an institution/university recognized by the BCI; fulfills such other conditions as may be specified in the rules made by the State Bar Council; and has paid, in respect of the enrolment, stamp duty, if any, and an enrolment fee payable to the State Bar Council. It is to be noted that a national of any other country may be admitted as an advocate on a state roll, if citizens of India, duly qualified, are permitted to practice law in that other country.

Apart from the above-mentioned conditions, the BCI in 2010 has mandated that law students are required to qualify in the All India Bar Examination (AIBE) in order to be enrolled as an advocate.

The purpose of this exam is to ensure that the quality of the Bar in India is increased by enforcing a minimum benchmark for law students seeking to practice across the country. The BCI in 2014 also mandated that the Certificate of Practice issued to an advocate shall be valid for a period of five years only and shall be renewed every five years by filing an application for renewal in advance. This should be done within a period of six months before the validity period of the "Certificate of Practice" or its renewal, expires.

As mentioned earlier, 'Advocates' is the only recognized class of persons entitled to practice law in India. Every advocate whose name is entered in the state roll is entitled to practice in all courts including the Supreme Court; before any tribunal or person legally authorized to take evidence; and before any other authority or person before whom such advocates are entitled to practice. However, the 2014 rule of the BCI introduced the requirement of minimum experience in subordinate courts in order to practice before higher courts of law.

An important consideration in all legal jurisdictions is how the 'practice of law' is defined in their respective jurisdiction. The Indian legal system also defines the 'practice of law' and the same has been clarified by courts in various cases involving what constitutes 'practice of law' in India. 'Practice of law' means and includes practicing before the court, tribunal, authority, regulator, administrative body or officer and any quasi-judicial and administrative body; giving legal advice either individually or from a law firm either orally or in writing; giving legal advice to any government, international body or representing any international dispute resolution bodies including International Court of Justice; engaging in legal drafting and participating in any legal proceedings; and representing in arbitration proceedings or any other alternative dispute resolution approved by law.

The Advocates Act also talks about reciprocity with regard to the practice of law in other country by Indian legal professionals. If any country, specified by the central government, prevents citizens of India from practicing the profession of law or subjects them to unfair discrimination in that country, no subject of any such country is entitled to practice the profession of law in India. However, the BCI may prescribe the conditions subject to which foreign qualifications in law obtained by persons other than citizens of India shall be recognized for the purpose of admission as an advocate.

Though most of the powers are vested in the BCI, it is worth noting that the central government may make rules including rules with respect to any matter for which the BCI or a State Bar Council has power to make rules. Such rules may provide for qualifications for membership of a Bar Council and disqualification from such a membership; the class or category of persons entitled to be enrolled as advocates under this Act; and the category of persons who may be exempted from undergoing a course of training and passing an examination; among others.

The BCI Rules, 1975[7]

The BCI has framed rules for maintaining professional standards in legal services in India by virtue of powers given to it under the Advocates Act. These rules relate to professional conduct, legal education, recognition of qualifications, advertising, etc. The State Bar Council council are required to enroll as advocate only such candidates, who have passed from university, approved affiliated Centre of Legal Education/Departments of the recognized University as approved by the BCI. These rules provide for two courses of law leading to bachelors degree in law, a three-year degree course in law undertaken after obtaining a bachelors' degree in any discipline of studies and the second, a double degree integrated course combining bachelors' degree course together with the bachelors' degree course in law, not less than five years in duration, leading to the integrated degree in the respective discipline of knowledge and law together.

The BCI rules also talk about the recognition of foreign degree by an Indian. If an Indian national obtains a degree in law from a foreign university, such a degree can be recognized for the purpose of enrolment on fulfillment of two conditions. First, the person

---

[7] Based on information available in the various Chapters of the BCI Rules, 1975, available at http://www.barcouncilofindia.org/about/professional-standards/rules-on-professional-standards/ (last accessed on January 1, 2015).

should have completed and obtained the degree in law after regularly pursuing the course for a period not less than three years in case the degree in law is obtained after graduation, or for a period of not less than five years if admitted into the integrated course after passing the higher secondary examination or its equivalent; and second, the university must be recognized by the BCI and the candidate concerned must pass the examination conducted by the BCI in substantive and procedural law subjects, which are specifically needed to practice law in India as prescribed by the BCI from time to time. The BCI on the recommendation of the Legal Education Committee may consider the application of a foreign University to enlist its name so that its law degree if obtained by an Indian can be considered for enrolment purpose.

The previous chapter outlines various regulations which are present in the legal services sector across the globe. Advertising is one such regulation. The BCI has also prescribed rules regarding advertising by legal professionals in India. According to these rules, an advocate shall not solicit work or advertise, either directly or indirectly, whether by circulars, advertisements, touts, personal communications, interviews not warranted by personal relations, furnishing or inspiring newspaper comments or producing his photographs to be published in connection with cases in which he/she has been engaged or concerned. Apart from this, his sign-board or name-plate should be of a reasonable size. The sign-board or name-plate or stationery should not indicate that he is or has been president or member of a Bar Council or of any association or that he has been associated with any person or organization or with any particular cause or matter or that he specializes in any particular type of work or that he has been a judge or an advocate general.

However, advocates can furnish information on the web site as prescribed and approved by the BCI. Any additional input on particulars other than those approved by the BCI will be deemed to be in violation of the BCI Rules and such advocates are liable to be proceeded against on the grounds of misconduct.

The BCI Rules also stipulate conditions for right to practice of an advocate. An advocate cannot enter into a partnership or any other arrangement for sharing remuneration with any person or legal practitioner who is not an advocate. Apart from this, no advocate enrolled under the Advocates Act is entitled to practice unless such an advocate successfully passes the AIBE conducted by the BCI. The AIBE is mandatory for all law students graduating from academic year 2009–2010 onward who wish to get enrolled as advocates under the Advocates Act. The AIBE is required to be conducted by the BCI at least twice each year in such month and such places that the BCI may determine from time to time.

It is also to be noted that the BCI rules allow a practicing advocate to take up teaching of law in any educational institution which is affiliated to a university. However, the hours during which he/she is so engaged in the teaching of law should not exceed three hours in a day. If an advocate is employed in any such educational institution for the teaching of law and if the hours during which he/she is so engaged do not exceed three hours, such employment shall be deemed to be part-time employment.

Comparing Indian Regulatory Environment with Selected Countries

As most of the issues discussed in the previous section pertain to the regulatory framework and aspects such as entry, training, standards, and practices, it is important to benchmark India with other countries to see to what extent it differs in its regulatory practices and where its shortcomings lie, keeping in view the global norms. The following discussion highlights the differences that emerge from an examination of the regulatory environment in selected countries.

Regulatory Framework

A comparative analysis of the regulatory framework in this sector across different countries indicates that the sector is regulated by a mix of government (under a designated ministry), a professional body constituted by member practitioners from the sector, various councils and commissions consisting of independent sectoral experts, academics and government officials either under some overarching legislation, or a government ministry. While India's regulatory setup broadly lies within the spectrum of regulatory possibilities, it differs in one important respect. It tends to concentrate authority much more than other countries in a single regulatory body. As mentioned earlier, several of the countries examined in this study have separate boards and councils which are responsible for different regulatory functions within the sector.

Thus clearly, the regulatory structure in other countries attempts to (a) minimize conflicts of interest that could arise when a regulator performs multiple functions; (b) enhance the efficiency of the regulatory framework by creating sub-regulatory structures; (c) align regulatory capabilities with the functions undertaken; and (d) provide an independent and informed review of regulatory reform issues (such as by creating independent commissions/bodies). Most countries have multiple independent oversight bodies set up under government ministries or under an overarching Law Society or Association, which are responsible for issues such as registration, adherence to codes of conduct, and ethics. So, the key difference between India and other countries is that the latter tend to have a more layered approach to regulation and governance, wherein regulatory authority is more dispersed and customized to suit different requirements within the profession.

The Indian regulatory framework also differs from that of other larger countries like the US where State Bar Associations have the jurisdiction over registration and licensing, whereas in India, the State Bar Councils are largely chapters of the central regulatory body, but do not have separate licensing or disciplinary powers. Again, this reflects the centralized nature of the regulatory framework in India.

Training and Capacity Building

An overview of the training requirements across countries indicates the importance given by most countries to CPD and re-certification. As discussed earlier, in Malaysia, specific rules have been developed recently mandating CPD with provisions for periodic updating.

In Singapore, advocates and solicitors admitted to the Bar post 2007 must meet the CPD requirements. Australia too has CPD requirements for both barristers and solicitors. In the UK, there is a system of continuing exams and every year, the license has to be renewed. Courses have to be attended and a minimum number of points must be collected in order to renew the license. Thus, clearly there is emphasis on keeping up to date, periodic honing of skills, and ensuring quality along with provisions for upgrading of curricula and formats for professional development. India falls short in this respect, in addition to the problems such as the poor quality of its legal training and lack of standardization in licensing.[8]

Another area where India's legal training and education falls short is practical training. There is emphasis on pupillage, clerkship, apprenticeship, vocational education following graduation in many countries (e.g., Malaysia, China, Singapore, and Australia) for periods ranging from six months to two years in some cases. The lack of applied orientation in training is also borne out by a cross-country examination of training and qualification requirements.

Restrictions on Domestic Firms

A cross-country review of the regulations concerning advertising and soliciting of business by legal professionals shows that this is largely permitted, subject to limited conditions. Lawyers are allowed to advertise provided they do not make exaggerated claims or use negative publicity about other professionals or firms in their sector. Communication via different media (electronic, mass, printed form) is permitted in several countries for raising public awareness, building a client relationship, and for educating the public. India, however as mentioned earlier, is more restrictive in the area of advertising compared to other countries. Only limited websites can be maintained. (It is a different matter that there are alleged violations of this restriction and the enforcement seems to be poor.)

---

[8] It is only recently in 2010 that an All India Bar Exam has been introduced to qualify for legal practice in India.

An examination of the provisions on LLPs suggests that there is ambiguity in several countries. In India too, while LLPs are permitted, associated changes in the Advocates Act and BCI rules have not been made and thus LLPs may not be possible in legal services.[9] In some countries such as Malaysia and Japan, LLPs are allowed but there is lack of clarity on how LLPs would operate in the sector. In some cases like China, LLPs are only permitted with domestic firms. Thus, the status of LLP in India does not seem to be too different from that in other developing countries, indicating that the sector is still evolving with respect to these different forms of partnership and that an understanding of the implications of LLPs for foreign participation, taxation, insurance, scope of operations, and other operations is still nascent in many countries.[10]

Regulations on Foreign Firms

A cross-country examination of the rules regarding foreign firms indicates that there are many limitations on their participation across all countries. The most common restriction is on the scope of practice, wherein foreign firms are limited to the practice of international and home country law and are not allowed to practice domestic (host country) law. In addition, some countries limit particular activities such as litigation, drawing up court documents, immigration services, and property transfer to nationals. Thus clearly, jurisdiction is an important natural barrier that is used to carve out the market and to limit competition for domestic firms.

There are also direct and indirect restrictions on the employment of local lawyers. In Singapore for instance, a FLF is not permitted to employ a qualified Singaporean lawyer, while in China, a licensed Chinese lawyer has to suspend his/her license and cannot practice domestic law while employed at an international law firm in China. Such conditions aim at preventing the loss of domestic

---

[9] There is lot of confusion about the LLP format. It is possible that additional regulations may come into play which would allow FLFs to form an LLP with an Indian law firm subject to one of the partners must be a resident in India.

[10] See the note on the Indian LLP law by Sachdeva and Sachdeva (2009), p. 6.

talent to foreign firms and at creating a clear divide in the scope of practice between domestic and FLFs (as otherwise there can be a blurring of these jurisdictional boundaries when foreign firms employ domestic lawyers). Some countries also specify conditions on holding of shares in local law firms. Some host countries require FLFs to justify commercial presence on economic and social grounds and to wait for some years before they are allowed to open additional offices in that market. Residency conditions are also imposed on FLFs, such as requiring a partner of a foreign firm to be present in the country for a minimum specified period in a year, as in the case of Malaysia. There is also discriminatory treatment of FLFs, such as through double taxation of profits and taxes being applied at a higher rate than for domestic law firms, as in the case of China. In some countries like the US, eligibility to practice depends on state level regulations and visa and residency conditions. Thus, commercial presence, even if allowed in principle, is subject to many visible and not so visible conditions and is permitted only in a gradual, calibrated manner across countries.

It is also interesting to note that there is a lot of emphasis on the governance of foreign legal practice. It is clearly specified in several countries that FLFs would be subject to all applicable domestic laws governing the legal profession and that the host country regulator would have control over the operations of foreign firms. In this context, some countries like Australia specifically state that establishment of an office or carrying out of business by a FLF or by a foreign legal professional is only possible if the latter has been recognized as a firm or as an accredited lawyer in Australia. This implies that the regulatory framework of countries is cognizant of the need to bring foreign firms and professionals under their governance ambit. They do this by formally recognizing the firms and the professionals, which then enables them to subject these entities/individuals to domestic disciplines. Such governance is an extension of the strict checks on domestic firms. There is regular auditing of law firms in many countries, transactions have to be reported, and standards of practice have to be maintained. Thus, governance of both domestic and foreign firms is an important role of the regulator in other countries.

The main difference that emerges between India and the other countries examined earlier is that India does not allow FLFs to practice in its market through establishments while the others do, through JVs or through representative offices or equity participation.[11] However, the cross-country review of regulatory practices shows that all countries maintain a variety of conditions on foreign firms even if they allow entry at the border. Through these "behind-the-border" regulatory conditions, they can significantly limit the operations of foreign firms and address possible negative fallouts of foreign commercial presence.

India's Trade in Legal Services

Though legal services sector is one of the most restrictive sectors in India, legal services exports and imports of India have witnessed a significant increase over the past few years. According to the services trade database of the United Nations (UN), India's legal services exports and imports increased from 2004 to 2008 but declined in 2009 and 2010. The UN database does not have such data for India beyond year 2010. Figure 4.1 and Table 4.1 provide information on India's legal services exports and imports for the 2004–2010 period.

Figure 4.1 and Table 4.1 clearly show that India's legal services exports are significantly higher than its legal services imports for the 2004–2010 period, except in 2004. Both exports and imports have shown an identical upward trend till 2008, falling thereafter. The decline after 2008 can be attributed to a general slump in economic and business activities after the global financial crisis.

---

[11] The primary survey carried out during this study revealed that on a continuum from the least to the most restrictive legal sector, India is the most restrictive. China and Brazil allow FLFs to establish an office but only to practice foreign law, while Russia is more liberal as one can practice both foreign and local law.

Figure 4.1
India's Legal Services Exports and Imports (in US$ Millions), 2004–2010

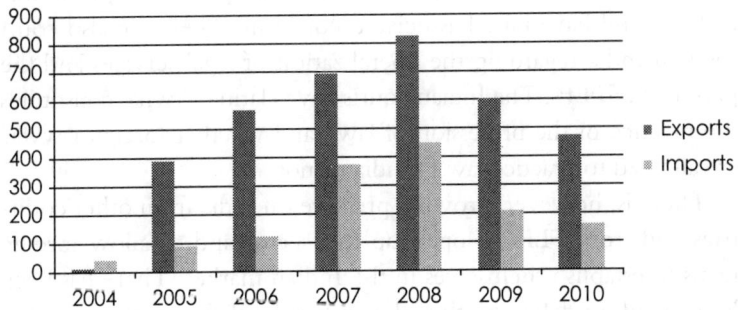

Source: Authors' construction based on UN Services Trade Database.

Table 4.1
India's Legal Services Exports and Imports (in US$ Millions), 2004–2010

Period	Exports	Imports
2004	15	43
2005	388	88
2006	562	122
2007	691	373
2008	823	448
2009	603	212
2010	474	160

Source: UN Services Trade Database.

India's Approach toward Liberalizing Legal Services

Liberalization of legal services is a very hotly contested issue in India. India's approach to opening up its legal services market can be termed defensive and restrictive. In various debates concerning liberalizing the Indian economy, legal services usually do not find mention and such debates remain limited to services such as retail, financial, telecommunications, etc. However, there are some studies and books that have discussed the opening up of legal services in India and have raised associated concerns. There are also court cases in India regarding the liberalization of legal services and the presence of FLFs. The Indian courts have clarified "what constitutes the practice of the profession of law" and whether foreign lawyers are allowed to practice law in India or not.

There is, however, growing pressure on India from other countries and from FLFs to open up this sector and to allow foreign firms to establish themselves in the Indian market. There has been long standing debate within the Indian legal fraternity about the desirability of opening up and its likely impact on Indian law firms, Indian legal professionals, and Indian businesses and clients. Several interesting issues have emerged in the course of this debate, though many of these are not clear cut and often tend to be colored by the interests of different stakeholders and by biased perceptions.

In addition to the domestic regulations mentioned earlier which affect the operations of domestic law firms, another major regulation pertains to foreign commercial presence or FDI in this sector. FDI is not permitted in legal services in India. Thus, FLFs cannot establish a commercial presence in India and are prohibited from giving any legal advice that could constitute practice of Indian law. Indian advocates are also not permitted to enter into profit sharing arrangements with persons other than Indian advocates.

Presence of Foreign Law Firms in India

The history of the presence of FLFs in India can be traced back to the 1990s when Ashurst, Chadbourne, and Parke, and White and Case opened up their liaison offices in India after the RBI gave them permission to do so under the Foreign Exchange Regulation Act, 1973. However, the 'Lawyers Collective'[12] alleged that these firms were involved in legal practice and giving consultancy

---

[12] "Lawyers Collective" is a society registered under the Societies Registration Act and under the Bombay Public Trusts Act.

legal services instead of operating only as liaison offices. In accordance with this viewpoint, the 'Lawyers Collective' had filed a writ petition as a Public Interest Litigation in the Bombay High Court in 1995. Two questions were raised in this petition; first, whether the permissions granted by the Reserve Bank of India (RBI) to the above-mentioned FLFs to establish liaison office in India under Section 29 of the Foreign Exchange Regulation Act, 1973, were legal and valid; and second, whether these FLFs could carry on their liaison activities in India only on being enrolled as advocates under the Advocates Act, 1961, i.e., whether practicing in non-litigious matters amounted to 'practicing the profession of law' under Section 29 of the Advocates Act, 1961.

Hearing the petition, the Bombay High Court, at the interim stage, held that the words 'to practice the profession of law' have a very wide mandate and include advisory services. Hence, the FLFs, by providing such services, were in fact practicing law in India. The High Court also noted that only an Indian citizen could be an advocate under the Advocates Act. The matter was subsequently appealed, and it came before the Supreme Court of India in March 1996. The Supreme Court did not decide on the substantive issue and remanded back the matter to the Bombay High Court (Based on Hariani 2010).

The Bombay High Court in December 2009 held that the RBI was not justified in granting permission to the FLFs to open liaison offices in India under Section 29 of the 1973 Act. The judgment stated that

> It appears that before approaching RBI, these foreign law firms had approached the Foreign Investment Promotion Board (FIPB for short) a High Powered body established under the New Industrial Policy seeking their approval in the matter. The FIPB had rejected the proposal submitted by the foreign law firms. Thereafter, these law firms sought approval from RBI and RBI granted the approval in spite of the rejection of FIPB. Though specific grievance to that effect is made in the petition, the RBI has chosen not to deal with those grievances in its affidavit in reply. Thus, in the present case, apparently, the stand taken by RBI and FIPB is mutually contradictory. (Judgment—W.P.1526/1995, in the High Court of Judicature at Bombay, Writ Petition No. 1526 of 1995, p. 29: para 44.)

The Bombay High Court further held that the expressions 'to practise the profession of law' in Section 29 of the Advocates Act, 1961, is wide enough to cover the persons practicing in litigious matters as well as persons practicing in non-litigious matters. Thus, to practice in non-litigious matters in India, the FLFs (as mentioned in the writ petition) were bound to follow the provisions contained in the 1961 Act.

A writ petition has also been filed by A.K. Balaji in 2010 in the Madras High Court under Article 226 of the Constitution of India for the issuance of a Writ of Mandamus directing the Government of India, the RBI, and the BCI to take appropriate action against FLFs or foreign lawyers, who are illegally practicing the profession of law in India. The petition also called for a further direction to prevent them from having any legal practice either on the litigation side or in the field of non-litigation and commercial transactions, in any manner whatsoever within the territory of India.

The Madras High Court's 2012 order did not disagree with the Bombay High Court regarding the practice of the profession of law in India by FLFs or foreign lawyers. However, it said that there is no bar on foreign lawyers to visit India on a "fly-in-fly-out" basis for the purpose of giving legal advice to their clients in India regarding foreign law or their own system of law and on diverse international legal issues. Foreign lawyers cannot be debarred from coming to India and conducting arbitration proceedings in respect of disputes arising out of a contract relating to international commercial arbitration. It also said that the business process outsourcing (BPO) companies providing a wide range of customized and integrated services and functions to its customers like word-processing, secretarial support, transcription services, proof-reading services, travel desk support services, etc., do not come within the purview of the Advocates Act, 1961, or the BCI Rules.

This matter reached the Supreme Court through an appeal by the BCI. It wanted the Supreme Court to clarify on the issue as the Madras High Court's 2012 judgment was contrary to the earlier ruling of the Bombay High Court that no foreign lawyers or firms can operate in India. The BCI maintained that various FLFs had set up their offices in India and were dealing with activities such as mergers, takeovers, acquisitions, amalgamations, and arbitrations including various commercial transactions. The BCI also maintained that the foreign lawyers come on visitor visas and conduct arbitration in Indian hotels and illegally involved in practising law.

The Supreme Court July 2012 Order clarified that the RBI shall not grant any permission to FLFs to open liaison offices in the country. It also clarified that the expression 'to practice the profession of law' under Section 29 of the Advocates Act, 1961 covers the persons practicing litigious matters as well as non-litigious matters.

Thus, it could be said that the FLFs are bound by the provisions of Section 29 of the Advocates Act, 1961. Without having an amendment to the said section of the 1961 Act, it may not be possible for the FLFs to operate in India.

India's Commitments on Legal Services under the GATS and Revised Offer

Legal services are part of 'business services' in the WTO classification of services. The legal services sector is one of those services in which very few countries have taken commitments. As mentioned earlier, according to the background note on legal services, WTO Secretariat (S/C/W/318, 2010), 76 members have taken commitments in legal services under the GATS.

As far as India's commitments in legal services are concerned, India has not scheduled the legal services sector in its Uruguay Round commitments or in its subsequent initial and revised offers under the WTO. It is worth mentioning that India received requests under the Doha Round of GATS negotiations to make binding commitments to allow foreign commercial presence in legal services, as many developed countries were very keen to have India opening up this sector. However, thus far, India has not offered any commitment to open legal services in its revised offer.

A closer analysis of commitments of various countries reveals that market access and national treatment are only partially granted in most of these commitments.[13] For market access commitments on commercial presence, the most common restrictions appearing in members' schedules are limitations on the type of legal entity permitted. In general, members have limited the choice of legal form to natural persons (sole proprietorship) or partnerships, thus excluding limited companies. In a few instances, partnerships have also been excluded. Other important limitations exist with regard to the Mode 4 commitments on contract service suppliers and independent professionals, which may severely restrict fly-in-fly-out services.

As far as national treatment restrictions are concerned, the majority of these are residency requirements. In some cases, these requirements are linked to a nationality requirement. There also exist local education requirements as national treatment restrictions in some of the members' schedule of commitments. Other scheduled national treatment restrictions include: (a) recognition of foreign degrees only for own nationals who have studied abroad; (b) the requirement that foreign ventures be competitive institutions in their country of origin; and (c) the requirement for foreign lawyers to take active part in the business in order to be able to maintain an interest in a local law firm.

India's Commitments on Legal Services under Its Free Trade Agreements

Free Trade Agreements (FTAs) in which India is involved can be broadly divided into two types, the ones which have been notified to WTO and those which have not been notified to the WTO.

---

[13] "Market access" refers to the extent to which foreign service providers are permitted entry into the market of the country scheduling the commitment. This could take the form of "none" meaning unrestricted access, "partial" meaning access which is partly restricted and subject to certain conditions, or "unbound" which means no commitment has been made. "National Treatment" refers to whether foreign service providers are treated at par with domestic service providers or whether there are any discriminatory provisions affecting their operations in the market of the country scheduling the commitment. This too can be unrestricted, partial, or uncommitted.

As per the WTO web site, India in total has notified to the WTO Secretariat 20 Regional Trade Agreements (RTAs).[14] Out of these, 4 are ongoing and the remaining 16 are settled and are in force. Out of the 16 which are settled, only 4 cover both services and goods. The remaining 12 cover only goods.

These 4 WTO notified RTAs which cover services are, *India–Japan*, *India–Malaysia*, *India–Singapore*, and *Republic of Korea–India*. In sync with its approach of not scheduling legal services in the GATS and in its revised offer, India has not scheduled legal services in its FTAs with these countries, though these countries have made partial commitments on legal services in these FTAs with India. In three of the four above-mentioned agreements, the other signatories have made partial commitments in legal services for India's legal service providers. These commitments are provided in Tables A.4–A.6.

India's Mutual Recognition Agreements

MRAs are one of the ways to overcome the restrictive regulatory environment arising from licensing and registration requirements that prevail in such accredited sectors. Whereas on one hand, such agreements allow increased foreign participation in the concerned service sector, on the other hand, they help in ensuring consumer safety and meeting public policy objectives, as the foreigners are allowed to provide their services only once their qualifications are validated by the country concerned through the provisions of the MRA. As far as MRAs are concerned, India has not signed any MRA in legal services. Though the BCI is of the opinion that the Indian legal profession cannot view itself in isolation from international practices and approaches in law, it has not been very active in negotiating MRAs with other countries. The BCI has so far entered into a memorandum of understanding with the Law Council of Australia and is putting in place a law student exchange program with the Paris Bar Association.

---

[14] RTAs include both FTAs and preferential trade agreements (PTAs). However, many times, FTA and RTA terms are used interchangeably.

Thus, it appears that India's approach to opening up of legal services has been rather restrictive as it has not scheduled legal services in its GATS commitments or in its initial and revised offers under the WTO or in its FTAs with other countries. Moreover, the MRA negotiations have not been significant in this sector. This approach could partially be attributed to the internal dynamics against liberalization of this sector in India.

5
Political Economy of Liberalization: Stakeholders' Views*

The preceding discussion has highlighted clearly the restrictive regulatory environment that characterizes India's legal services sector both at the border and behind-the-border. The sector is closed to FDI. There are a large number of domestic regulations concerning scale, scope, and operating conditions which constrain the growth, competitiveness, and internationalization of Indian law firms. The sensitivity surrounding the relaxation of some of these regulations is evident from India's reluctance to table legal services for liberalization both under the GATS negotiations and in its bilateral comprehensive economic cooperation and partnership arrangements. This stand has prevailed notwithstanding the growing pressure from the US and the UK to open up India's legal services sector and to address the growing need for expertise in corporate and international law in the Indian economy.

Available studies by academics and legal experts reflect the long standing nature of the debate within the Indian legal fraternity and the different perspectives regarding the desirability of opening up

---

*The views expressed in this chapter are those of the stakeholders and not of the authors. The 'Chatham House Rules' were being followed while soliciting the views of various stakeholders.

India's legal services sector and its likely impact on Indian law firms, Indian legal professionals, and Indian industry. Those who oppose liberalization of the sector argue that the entry of FLFs would make it difficult for small Indian law firms to survive and would hurt the common Indian by raising the cost of legal services. Fears of employment diversion of the best and brightest lawyers from Indian to higher paying FLFs also underlie this opposition to the presence of foreign firms in India. There is also a concern among a section of the legal fraternity that despite the restriction on foreign commercial presence, FLFs are already present in the Indian market through liaison offices and informal tie-ups with Indian firms and provide advisory services which are in breach of statutory requirements. The opposition has been strident. A section of Indian law firms has collectively formed a society of Indian Law firms and has actively campaigned against the entry of FLFs, given the prevailing regulatory environment which they claim puts Indian firms at a disadvantage in terms of size, scope, and operating conditions.

But, those who support greater competition and internationalization of the sector argue that opening up is inevitable and required by Indian businesses as the Indian economy becomes more globally integrated. In this view, the entry of FLFs would benefit Indian legal professionals by creating varied and better paid employment opportunities. It would also benefit Indian law firms through the transfer of knowledge, technology, and best practices, and by helping to develop specialized expertise. This section of the Indian legal fraternity also questions many of the negative fallouts associated with liberalization as being overblown and unlikely to materialize if a calibrated and phased approach is taken to opening up the sector.

Thus, the sector has been witness to much debate, with perhaps the critics of liberalization dominating the debate thus far. But increasingly, a more nuanced set of perspectives is emerging wherein the debate has shifted to taking stock of the shortcomings in the domestic regulatory framework and capacity and to understanding how best to prepare the sector for opening up, keeping in mind the market structure, public interest, and stakeholder sensitivities. What emerges clearly from these discussions is that the debate is influenced by political economy considerations and the interests of different stakeholders. It reflects a mix of both well-founded and biased views and perceptions, which are often hard to separate given the rather strident nature of some of the rhetoric that has tended to mark the debate over legal services liberalization in India.

This chapter provides an overview of the issues and concerns that pertain to this debate followed by a critical and objective analysis of the arguments and rationale, in part drawing upon the literature on regulation and liberalization of professional services discussed earlier. Such an approach is needed as any policy initiatives aimed at legal services reforms and liberalization will need to examine the opposing points of view and the different perspectives in order to arrive at a balanced assessment of the arguments on both sides and accordingly take steps, in the long-term interests of the sector and the Indian economy. As highlighted earlier, jurisdiction and sectorial studies are important for understanding the extent to which issues are specific to a profession, in this case legal services, and to what extent the debate resonates with that found in the general professional services literature. Such a distinction can enable one to understand whether sector-specific measures are needed or whether a set of common principles and regulatory approaches across a range of professional services would be more appropriate.

The discussion in this chapter is based on the findings from a small-scale survey that was carried out to solicit the views of a wide range of stakeholders and experts in the legal services sector regarding the regulatory and competitive challenges in this sector in India, and the implications of its liberalization for the sector and for the wider economy. The discussion highlights the concerns and sensitivities expressed by those surveyed and by participants at stakeholder consultations. Interspersed with the survey findings is a critique of some of the issues raised by respondents and how they relate to the literature on professional services and on legal services specifically. The discussion of survey results is followed by a critical analysis of some of the main points that emerge and an assessment of their validity, the reasons underlying these expressed views, the extent to which the latter are objectively grounded, and how the arguments presented fit within the broader analytical framework of professional services regulation and liberalization presented earlier.

Background to the Survey

In-depth discussions were carried out with practitioners in Indian and FLFs as well as a wide range of other representatives from the legal sector, over the June 2012–March 2013 period. A total of 20 such one-on-one discussions were conducted covering a representative set of stakeholders in the sector who could provide views from different perspectives. The respondents included a mix of large, medium, and small domestic firms, some proprietary and some family-owned, some having an affiliation with a FLF and others unaffiliated; government officials;[1] representatives from associations in India, the UK and the US, and academics and industry experts on legal services. The respondents from firms included partners and senior management. The respondents were based in Delhi, Bangalore, UK, and the US. The sample was mostly determined on the basis of contacts obtained by the authors from industry associations and their own networks and expanded using a snowball sampling approach. Of the contacts obtained, those who were amenable for discussion were chosen as respondents. The choice of locations was driven by two factors. Delhi was chosen due to the presence of some of the largest Indian firms as well as some boutique firms, the presence of regulators, government officials, and experts. Bangalore was chosen due to the availability of academics in law and some new firms with affiliation experience with foreign firms. The choice of the US and UK was based on the need to get the views of legal professionals and regulatory bodies in these countries given their significant role and contribution in shaping the debate over legal services regulation and liberalization in international forums. Attempts to interview law firms in Mumbai were unsuccessful. However, to the extent that all the major law firms

---

[1] Officials from the ministry of law and justice and the ministry of commerce were covered in the survey.

in India were covered in these discussions, some of them also having offices in other major Indian cities outside Delhi, the focus on a few cities is not a major limitation. The discussions were semi-structured and open-ended, typically lasting about an hour and were conducted in person and over the telephone.

The discussions focused on two broad and inter-related questions. The first concerned the regulatory environment and associated competitiveness challenges faced by firms in India's legal services sector. The second concerned the likely impact of opening up this sector on domestic players, on the sector as a whole and the longer term implications. Within these themes, a wide range of issues were addressed during the in-depth discussions. The topics covered included issues of market structure; regulatory, structural, and other constraints affecting the Indian legal services sector; the role and effectiveness of regulatory bodies; the current regulatory framework and recent regulatory developments in this sector; the implications of potential future opening up of legal services in India through FDI/JVs/partnerships between domestic and FLFs; modalities and operations of foreign firms in India and their regulatory status; barriers faced by Indian legal professionals in other markets; and required regulatory reforms and capacity building measures in light of emerging opportunities, global practices, and the need for strengthening this sector.

These discussions were supplemented by a roundtable discussion organized with the support of a leading industry association in New Delhi in October 2012. The consultation saw the participation of representatives from large and small Indian law firms, foreign firms, individual practitioners, industry clients making use of legal services and academics and experts knowledgeable about this sector. The roundtable enabled an open exchange of opinions and debate on the regulatory environment, the strengths and weaknesses of the sector, and the prospects for and challenges associated with reforming legal services in India. The roundtable in India was followed by roundtable in London in February 2013, where the views of foreign lawyers and Indian lawyers working in the UK were solicited. The findings from these discussions and roundtables were again presented in Delhi in March 2013 to a small group of legal experts and practitioners to further refine the analysis.

Although the survey findings were quite extensive given the open-ended nature of the in-depth discussions and the roundtable, the most salient issues that emerged centered around three main themes, namely, the regulatory, infrastructural, and institutional and structural factors that constrain the competitiveness of India's legal services sector; the degree of preparedness of the sector to confront the challenges posed by globalization; and the steps needed to strengthen and reform the sector in line with its long-term interests and the emerging needs of the Indian economy. Regulatory reforms and capacity building requirements thus featured among the central issues and concerns for stakeholders and thus provide the context within which the following discussion and analysis of the survey findings are presented.

The following sections of this chapter summarize the views that were expressed by stakeholders during the survey and roundtable discussions, first on the issues of regulation and second on the issue of liberalizing legal services. It is important to note at this juncture that the views expressed on these two issues, though presented here separately, are quite interdependent. As the discussion highlights, concerns about competitive challenges in the sector largely stem from the prevailing regulatory environment and market structure and it is these very challenges which also form the basis for concerns about the opening up of the sector. Hence, many of the arguments regarding regulation and liberalization of legal services must be understood as interwoven and as underpinning one another. As a result, similar issues do arise in the discussion on competitive challenges and in the discussion on liberalization as these views on each have a bearing on the other.

Views on Regulatory and Other Challenges to Competitiveness

A variety of policy induced as well as structural constraints that hurt the competitiveness of Indian law firms and professionals were highlighted in the course of the survey and discussions with stakeholders. The constraints that emerged can be classified under five categories: (a) regulatory barriers; (b) lack of preparedness and capacity, weaknesses in the regulatory structure, and associated problems of governance and enforcement; (c) lack of reciprocity and access to other markets; and (d) structural/inherent factors. The discussions also indicated that it is often these very issues that underlie the concerns expressed by Indian law firms and professionals about the opening up of legal services, even if this opening up pertains to only a limited set of segments in this sector.

Regulatory Barriers

A concern voiced by almost all stakeholders is the lack of a level playing field with FLFs on account of a restrictive regulatory environment in India. They noted regulatory constraints on marketing their services, on the scale and scope of their activities, and on the firm structure and liability. However, contrary views also emerged on some of these same regulatory aspects indicating that not all stakeholders see these as constraining factors. The following discussion presents both points of view on selected regulatory issues.

Advertising Restrictions

The most commonly voiced constraint is the inability of Indian firms to advertise their services on account of the restrictions on advertising under the Advocates Act. In the past, Indian law firms have not been allowed to directly market themselves and only third party information and word of mouth referrals have been the means to advertise expertise. Law firms which put out any information have often received a show cause notice. This restriction stems from the view that legal services are a profession and not a business and thus marketing and solicitation should not be permitted. But increasingly, the view that is emerging is that the latter is an archaic notion, and that the approach to advertising has evolved in most countries given a shift in thinking about legal services from being only a profession to also being a business, and today to also being a service. Hence, India's regulatory approach to advertising must also reflect this change in thinking worldwide about the profession when it comes to advertising rules.

Although in recent years there has been some relaxation of these advertising restrictions with Indian law firms now being allowed to put some information online and the regulator recognizing some degree of marketing as acceptable and required for competition, there still remain ambiguities and limitations. Domestic firms can only put the name of the partner, the year of establishment, and their basic contact details, but they cannot showcase the experience and expertise of their partner/s, and they cannot bring out a brochure about the firm or put details on the web site. Soliciting thus remains a gray area given ambiguities about what is permissible to advertise and what is not. Hence, as some respondents noted, law firms which do not want to get into problems with the regulator do not rely on advertising to market their services and some firms may take it to the extreme of not even talking about their work. In contrast, foreign firms can advertise in magazines, television, the Internet, bring out brochures, and can provide detailed information about their past work and expertise. The UK law firms advertise in magazines of the Law Society of England and Wales. As foreign firms often have an established brand name, according to several Indian law firms who participated in the discussions, the inability of Indian firms to advertise and solicit business only puts them at a further disadvantage vis-à-vis foreign firms.

Most Indian respondents, across large and small firms noted that the regulations on advertising are outdated and do not serve their purpose, especially in an era of technology and Internet when monitoring such restrictions is difficult. Furthermore, there are violations of this restriction with some firms openly advertising on the Internet and through surrogate advertising. Deals are struck by law firms by advertising what they have done. Often firms provide more than the basic information online in their websites, like giving the client name and the transactions they have undertaken, and some have elaborate websites with disclaimers. False claims may be happening as well. All this implies that it is not possible to control advertising fully. The existing regulation on advertising is ineffective and it is increasingly difficult to monitor compliance.

Although the majority of respondents are critical about the advertising regulations and the uneven playing field they create for Indian firms, a small section of stakeholders expressed contrary views about the significance of advertising regulations for Indian law firms. In this view, advertising restrictions are not a critical challenge to the competitiveness of Indian law firms and professionals, as lawyers are 'professionals' not 'business persons', and 'professionals' do not self-advertise. Thus, reputation and expertise developed from past experience itself are sufficient, and advertising is typically not so important, in this view. Practitioners in some of the leading Indian law firms also echoed the latter view. Several mentioned that advertising and solicitation are not that important in this profession and that many lawyers do not use the advertising provision even in its relaxed form. This is because clients seek a professional relationship. They do not give work to firms on the basis of advertisements but rather on the basis of reputation, trust, and references. Moreover, marketing and solicitation can happen indirectly and this is permitted, such as through presence on panels, seminars, and other public events, and by providing information in noncompetitive ways (i.e., not doing active solicitation or comparative advertising or claim specializations). Hence, in the view of some professionals, especially those from the large, well-known Indian firms, the existing advertising restrictions are not that much of an impediment and are not critical to the process of getting work as personal branding is often more important. Further, as was pointed out by several respondents, the recent relaxation of restrictions on advertising and flexibilities given make the issue less of a binding constraint (although direct solicitation of business or providing specific information is still not permitted).

However, the general view was that the advertising restriction does not serve its purpose and could be removed. But for this, the Advocates Act must be amended and the issue has to be taken up proactively by the regulator, and domestic lawyers must put pressure on the regulator to initiate this change. The society of Indian Law firms has filed with the regulator to permit advertising on websites and certain kinds of promotions. Respondents also stated that in other developing countries such as Kenya where advertising restrictions are present, it is the domestic lawyers who have demanded the removal of the restriction. A similar push is required in India. Removal of the advertising restrictions would enable domestic lawyers to showcase their capabilities and businesses and thus create a level playing field vis-à-vis foreign firms. If other services such as insurance can benefit from marketing, then so can the legal sector.

It is interesting to note that the views expressed regarding the need and relevance of advertising restrictions in legal services echo the arguments contained in studies on professional services and debates that have taken place in markets like the US and the UK on the issue of competition, specifically with respect to regulations concerning advertising, soliciting, and other means of attracting clients. These studies, while noting the importance of reputation and trust in sectors like legal services also point out the competition limiting effects of advertising restrictions. Although advertising cannot fully correct the information problem and may also increase entry costs, there has been a rethink on advertising regulations in recognition of potential benefits that can arise from improved information flows about the services available in the market and differences in quality among providers, reduced search costs, and increased incentive to innovate. Evidence on the effects of advertising on competition and the level of fees in a market generally supports the view that more advertising increases competition within the profession and leads to lower fees, suggesting that relaxation of advertising restrictions is beneficial to consumers. The views expressed by the respondents on this issue indicate that the Indian legal services sector is at a juncture similar to that experienced by the legal profession in other countries on this issue two decades ago, and that the debate is still evolving.

Scale, Scope, and Liability Restrictions

Discussions with Indian law firms also threw up the issue of scale- and scope-related limitations which put Indian firms at a competitive disadvantage. At the time of conducting the survey, the number of partners permitted in Indian partnership firms was limited to 20 which in the view of respondents was preventing consolidation and scaling up in the sector. Further, advocates are not allowed to partner with and to share fees with non-advocates. There are thus two sets of restrictions, one affecting the size of the firm and another affecting the scope of its activities.

Some respondents stated that they would like the limitation on the number of partners to be removed (it got removed with the introduction of the Companies Act, 2013). Some also wanted the restriction on MDPs under the Advocates Act to be relaxed so that lawyers could partner with other professionals such as accountants and management consultants and the merging of such firms would become possible. The need for multidisciplinary formats they stated is evident from the fact that some law firms are now hiring Chartered Accountants (CAs) without sharing profits with them and thus are working around the restrictions. Allowing such partnerships would enable these firms to take on larger volumes of business and to earn higher revenues.

Once again, however, there were opposing views on both these issues. With regard to scale and partnership restrictions, some respondents questioned whether it is indeed a major constraint on competitiveness. Some of the smaller firms noted that the partnership limit provides space in the sector for small firms, which might otherwise have been forced to exit. They argued that if the restrictions are removed, then opportunities will also be reduced for the smaller firms to establish themselves. Hence, the limitation on the number of partners fulfills a social purpose by allowing the small firms to survive and to serve a certain segment of the Indian clientele.

There was also some skepticism about the need for law firms to become bigger and consolidate as it was felt that the sector could become less competitive and oligopolistic in nature and that quality could suffer if there were fewer firms. It was argued that unlike the case of goods, in services, there is no clear justification for consolidation and for economies of scale and scope as service quality may improve with many small players and a more competitive structure. Further, it was noted that many small Indian firms handle a large number of projects and that their turnover or size has not affected their ability to compete for large projects. Family firms have also become more specialized over time and many firms have developed their niche markets. Hence, some respondents felt that issues of scale, number of partners, consolidation, etc. cannot be directly linked to competence and quality. Several respondents also mentioned that the limitation on the number of partners is not as restrictive as it is made out to be. Some firms have got around the scale restriction by setting up separate offices, while keeping the common brand name. They work on a retainer basis and are part of a multifirm setup. They get a fixed retainer fee and the partner is in charge of the revenues. They do not share profits and thus avoid conflicts of interest and any violation of the Advocates Act. So the partnership limit can be overcome if firms want to scale up.

Another important point regarding whether scale restrictions are a binding constraint or not was that despite having a regulatory limit of 20 partners per firm, even before the enactment of the Companies Act, 2013, some 95 percent of the sector was made up of single proprietorship firms. Further, there are very few real partnerships, maybe less than 5 percent of all firms. None of the big Indian firms have reached a size of 20 partners. Hence, the partnership restriction may not be as binding a constraint in reality and there may be other underlying factors which are inhibiting the scaling up of Indian firms.

Discussions to probe these underlying constraints did indeed reveal other factors which are affecting the growth of Indian law firms possibly more than the aforementioned regulatory restrictions on scale. One of these reasons is *mindset and attitude*. There is a perception among Indian lawyers that becoming too big could affect service quality and can cause the firm to become a business entity rather than a service provider. It was pointed out by many respondents that Indian legal practitioners often prefer to offer personalized services and to retain flexibility in their operations and management practices, the type of work they do, and to keep control over quality. The unsuccessful experience of some leading Indian firms which tried to grow was cited to highlight the difficulties in controlling operations and quality in larger size firms.

It was noted that family-owned firms often choose not to increase the number of partners because they wish to keep the management within the family and would like to avoid conflicts of interest and problems that typically arise with having many partners.² As concerns the smaller firms, it was noted by some legal professionals and experts studying the sector that some of these firms choose to remain small or proprietary in nature because they are not too ambitious, or because the professionals want the firm to carry their name and are reluctant to grow and merge into a large firm where one has to be open to using general names and where there could be conflicts of interest with partners. Some respondents said that they preferred to stay out of partnerships as any bigger partner would want to dominate and they would lose their autonomy.³ Thus, there is an individualistic philosophy and culture which drives Indian law firms. Hence, a common view that emerged was that even when these firms have partners, these are not 'true' partnerships unless they are founding members of the firm. There are issues of relationship building and trust which keep Indian firms small on the whole.

Factors such as *attrition* were also cited as another reason why Indian law firms, small and big, choose not to take on many partners or take on many employees. Some respondents said that employees once trained, get the expertise but then quit and join another firm or set up their own firm. Hence, often firms prefer not to scale up or to convert their employees into partners as they are worried about the consequences if their partner quits. Family firms choose to pass on to the next generation within the family, so that they

---

² There were several critical comments in this regard. Many respondents pointed out that such an attitude of keeping the management within the family is not really conducive to building firms with modern practices. One respondent went so far as to say that non-family members have no chances in management of the company.

³ As put very strongly by one respondent, there is no segregation of ownership from management of the firm to running the business because Indian lawyers want to retain control over all aspects of the firm and this mindset is what prevents scaling and causes stagnation of business. There is need for consolidation through mergers and acquisitions.

can retain their expertise and niche. Thus, for a variety of reasons, many Indian lawyers prefer to work in small, self-owned firms, and family-owned firms do not take on outside partners. Scaling they said is important in the US model of a corporate law firm, but not in India where firms are not solely driven by revenues and the volume of business.[4] Hence, in the view of many respondents, it is not regulation that is the real impediment to size but it is 'mindset' and 'culture' that is restricting Indian law firms from growing.

The second underlying impediment to scale and growth in India's legal services sector concerns the *nature of the clientele in the Indian market and its paying capacity*. If firms have to grow much bigger, then they would need to be able to pass on their higher costs to their clients. But according to many respondents, most Indian client firms would not be in a position to pay such rates and those who can would go to the foreign firms given the latter's brand name and reputation and the variety of services they offer under one roof, which Indian firms may not be in a position to offer. As rates need to be reasonable for the majority of Indian clients who are small and have low paying capacity, domestic firms are likely to stay within the small- to mid-size segment. Thus, given the operating realities of the Indian market, it may not make sense for them to scale up to a very large size. There is a natural tendency for fragmentation and a segmented client profile within the Indian legal services sector.

Another structural constraint to growth pointed out by many respondents is the *lack of financial capital and infrastructure*. If Indian firms are to expand, consolidation must happen but this in turn requires investment in terms of space, financial capital, physical infrastructure, training, and standards, which most Indian professionals and small firms cannot afford.[5] However, Indian firms are

---

[4] For instance, a Boston Consulting Group (BCG) review found that the large Indian firms do not look at scaling in a strategic way, unlike corporate firms.

[5] It was noted by several respondents that due to the lack of financial capital, many Indian law firms operate out of residential basements and lack proper offices. Many law firms have set up offices in industrial or agricultural zones rather than in commercial spaces as they lack financing for taking commercial space.

not in a situation to adopt the business model of the FLFs as they lack the physical, financial, and human resources to do so, and also lack a supportive regulatory setup to access capital. They face cash flow and sustainability issues. Such financial and infrastructural constraints affect the ability of Indian firms to pay high salaries, or to put in place systems for growth and to build their brand name. Indian law firms cannot access credit from banks and need to rely on their retained earnings. As a result, Indian firms which have the potential to scale up and to compete globally in future are unable to. It was mentioned that some firms are working around these constraints by tying up with international firms or by using the legal process outsourcing (LPO) model. While FLFs operate like an industry and have access to huge amounts in loans (as much as US$100 million), Indian law firms are not recognized as an industry and thus lack access to capital. Some of the larger firms, however, noted that financing is not a major constraint as their retained earnings are significant and this problem may be pertinent only to the small proprietary firms.

On the issue of scope of practice and MDPs, there were also contrary views with some respondents stating that the Indian client base is still too small for such entities and that although there are synergies between legal services and other professions, the former is a very specialized profession which would not work well in an MDP format. Some prominent practitioners also stated that it may be better to keep professions separate as law is very different from all other professions in that it is proprietary in nature, based on individual competence and interpretation and thus conflicts of interest are highly likely if there are MDPs and very large firms. They also pointed out that not all jurisdictions allow MDPs, though cross-sectoral advice may be useful. Moreover, in their view many issues such as revenue sharing, modalities, liability, etc. would have to be addressed when forming MDPs. Several respondents noted that MDP firms are already in operation wherein firms have created divisions within the firm to separate different kinds of work across professions. One division can consist only of advocates. Law firms are opening tax departments and hiring CAs.

As long as there is no sharing of fees between advocates and non-advocates, there is no violation of the Advocates Act.[6] So, the restrictions on MDPs are not a major binding constraint to the competitiveness of Indian firms.

The issue of liability was raised by many respondents. The recent passage of the LLP Act, 2008, which permits LLPs, is expected to help Indian firms in several professional services to overcome the scale restrictions by enabling them to increase the number of partners while allowing them to restrict the extent of their liability. It is also generally felt that this development could give a boost to the setting up of MDPs and expanding the scope of their operations in sectors such as accountancy services. However, with reference to legal services, views were mixed regarding the extent to which LLPs would be initiated in the legal profession and also the need for such a liability structure in this profession.

One set of respondents argued that LLPs could potentially benefit the legal profession by enabling larger firms, with less risk borne by individual partners, particularly if this facilitated LLPs between legal professionals and professionals from other sectors, such as accountants and management consultants. However, they noted that such benefits cannot be realized in India's legal services sector unless corresponding changes are implemented in the Advocates Act as the latter does not permit partnerships with professionals in other sectors. Unless the Advocates Act permits MDPs, an LLP format may not have significance for the legal profession. Respondents also pointed out that in order to realize the potential benefits of an LLP structure, certain other supporting regulations would be needed and certain ambiguities in the existing regulations would need to be addressed. For instance, they highlighted the lack of clarity about how liability would be dealt given the regulator in legal services takes action against professionals and not firms and there is no corresponding concept of a corporate firm in the legal sector. Thus far, the regulator has not clarified how LLP firms would be treated.

---

[6] Examples of such cases were given where lawyers and CAs have come together on specific issues. Accounting firms also have legal cells.

Likewise, for converting into an LLP, there would be tax and revenue sharing implications and this would require corresponding changes in the Advocates Act. Supporting regulations would also be needed across state governments, regulators, and government departments, and agencies for LLPs to take off at an operational level. The current form of the LLP is thus seen to be made for corporate India, not the legal services sector. The net result of the absence of LLPs in legal services according to some stakeholders is that Indian firms are put at a competitive disadvantage vis-à-vis foreign firms as they do not have recourse to sue their partners for recovery of dues and are not able to compete with international law firms which have LLPs.

There was, however, an opposing view on the significance of LLPs in India's legal services sector and whether the current restrictions that make it difficult to form LLPs are really a binding constraint on organizational structure, scale, and scope of Indian law firms. The basis for this skepticism was that most Indian law firms, which are small in size and which survive on small business, like filing affidavits and *challans* (official form or document, such as an invoice, receipt or summons), would not be interested in LLPs. They would also not want to lose their autonomy under LLPs. Furthermore, as law is highly interpretive, like a trade secret, and partnerships must be based on trust, familiarity, and long-term relationships and not just business motives, it was felt that Indian firms may not want to enter into LLPs even if these were permitted. Some also noted that liability is not a major issue for Indian lawyers as they are not sued for wrong advice, unlike in the West. Further, contracts are subject to liability and so an LLP format may not be essential. Hence, for a variety of reasons, even in the forward looking firms, some respondents pointed out that LLPs are not likely to take off even if supporting regulations were amended and ambiguities addressed, as there would be little perceived benefit from forming such partnerships. On the whole, while many of those interviewed accepted that LLPs could potentially help domestic law firms in terms of building capacity, networking, and giving protection; it is not something they see as happening in India's legal services sector in the near future and also not a fundamental issue holding back the sector's competitiveness at present.

If one reflects on the various regulations affecting the organizational format, scale, and scope of practice in India's legal profession and the associated concerns voiced by the respondents, one finds that these are not unique to India. In almost all jurisdictions, such restrictions exist. Lawyers may be restricted to practicing as sole practitioners. They may be permitted to practice in groups, either only with lawyers or also with other professionals but the practice may be limited to partnerships with or without limited liability, or corporate forms may be allowed but with ownership restricted to members of the legal profession. The mixed views expressed by respondents suggest that it is difficult to say to what extent these restrictions on scale, scope, and liability structure are hurting the competitiveness of Indian law firms, especially given the fact that none of these appear to be binding constraints.

However, if one were to leave aside the issues of market structure, mindset, the absence of supporting regulatory amendments, and other such factors that make these regulations nonbinding, and if one were to draw upon the insights from the literature on the economics of regulation and organizational theory, then it would appear that the existing regulations are potentially hurting the growth and specialization of Indian law firms. Larger and multidisciplinary firms can reap the advantages of economies of scale, scope and specialization, and risk spreading, with resulting benefits in terms of improved quality and ability to sustain a lower cost for the same level of service. It can also be argued that allowing cross-disciplinary partnerships and external ownership of law firms, instead of creating a conflicting financial interest of the law firm owners as is often argued could actually work in the interests of the clients as the lawyer's financial interests may be less likely to interfere with his services than in the case of a proprietary or small partnership, lawyer-owned firm. Whether the removal or relaxation of the existing regulations would enable Indian law firms to realize these benefits or not given existing market conditions, finances, standards, and cultural factors is a different issue, but this does not deny the potential gains from relaxing some of these regulations.

Preparedness and Capacity

Perhaps more than some of the aforementioned regulatory restrictions, there was greater concern among stakeholders about how the sector's lack of preparedness and capacity makes it unable to face competition from foreign firms and from taking advantage of emerging global opportunities. Issues raised in this regard pertained to the standards and quality of legal education in the country and deficiencies in firm's capabilities and competence.

There was unanimity of views on the issue of training and standards. All those who participated in the survey, whether domestic or foreign, expressed concerns about the lack of rigor and deficiencies in India's legal education and training, excepting a few reputed National Law Schools which are more of a recent phenomenon. Many respondents noted that the quality of legal education and training is very weak in India and that the depth and quality of the available pool of legal professional is debatable. There is a problem of competence in the majority of law graduates. The weaknesses pointed out were numerous including: inadequate training and specialization, absence of revalidation mechanisms for licensing and registration to ensure updating and post studies training, absence of CLE, lack of practical orientation and professional exposure in the training program, failure to screen candidates rigorously through examinations, lack of emphasis on legal research, lack of rigor and professionalism in legal education, poor knowledge of English, and the large number of poor-quality law schools. The general view expressed was that most Indian law graduates lack specialized training and that the pool of available lawyers in emerging areas such as technology, infrastructure, IPR, competition policy, etc. remains very limited.

There were two common complaints about legal education and training across all those interviewed. The first was the lack of consistency in standards in law schools and the failure of the regulator to ensure quality, with consequent adverse effects on the overall quality of law graduates in the country. Many respondents noted that although thousands of law schools have received licenses to operate, some are very substandard while some are bogus and nonexistent. Many small colleges which are known to provide very poor-quality legal education are still given recognition by the regulator. Until recently, one could be employed in a law firm without clearing any all-India wide exam. It is only since 2010 that an all India Bar Exam has been introduced, which has to be cleared for eligibility to practice in court. But for corporate advisory services, there is still no standardized exam to screen for quality. It was further pointed out that the existing exams do not really focus on the quality of education or the substantive aspects of training and thus far do not serve as a screening device. This is unlike the case of accountancy services where the licensing exam has lot of credibility, both domestically and internationally, as a true quality check.

The second major deficiency voiced by most respondents was the lack of emphasis on CLE. As many pointed out, once a law degree is received, a law graduate can apply to the Local Bar Council at the state level and this gives him/her automatic membership. In the US, one needs to take an exam every few years to retain one's license, while in India though the renewing of license after every five years was made compulsory in 2014 by the BCI, such renewal is not based on any qualifying exam. One respondent also cited the lack of institutions in India which can help lawyers upgrade their skills and provide mid-career education.[7] Law firms are also not providing such training in-house for reasons of attrition and lack of orientation and mindset toward continuing education.

It was mentioned, however, that things are improving gradually, particularly with the establishment of more National Law Schools with five-year programs. These institutions are producing better quality graduates. However, some respondents stated that even these premier institutions need to improve by imparting more practical

---

[7] The example of one company was given as an institution that has been set up to improve the quality of lawyers in India.

orientation in their training, by focusing more on specialization, and by improving the quality of faculty, including getting practicing faculty. One positive development cited was the emergence of opportunities in the corporate law segment, which is helping to attract bright youngsters into the field. It is expected that with more exposure to international clients, standards will improve over time.

The aforementioned constraints which affect legal education and training in turn affect the capability of Indian law firms. Many respondents noted that Indian firms lack competence in that they do not have specialized expertise and domain knowledge, they do not focus on knowledge management, thought leadership, and in-house training. In contrast, foreign firms train their juniors, have knowledge databases, and emphasize upgrading of skills.

Overall, the general view was that Indian law firms cannot be globally competitive unless standards of training are upgraded in India. This requires much more emphasis to be placed on synergizing legal education with practice, to require periodic renewal of license through refresher courses and CLE, and for Indian law firms to have a more professional and modern outlook toward training and education. The education and training requirements and firm capabilities have to keep pace with emerging opportunities and domains.

These views were common across small, medium, and large law firms, those with and without foreign affiliations or aspirations. Thus the issue of training, standards, and quality clearly emerged as an area where proactive policies are needed on the part of the concerned ministry and the regulator. An interesting question that arises in this context is what would facilitate improved competitiveness of Indian law firms. Would exposure to more competition or improved standards of training and education or a combination of both enable this process? The answer to this question has to be nuanced and conditional on the existing market segmentation and conditions in India's legal services sector. Given the wide variability in training and the many lacunae in infrastructure, human resources, and regulation of quality, exposure to more competition is unlikely to help in raising general standards. Its effects may be limited to only a certain tier of training institutions and the benefits may accrue to only a certain tier of law firms which are in a position to adapt and employ such professionals. Hence, the focus has to be first on enforcing quality, upgrading skills, aligning training with market needs, with the dual benefit of strengthening the profession as a whole and enabling it to better withstand competitive pressures in the wake of liberalization.

Regulatory Framework and Governance Issues

As in the case of education and training, another area where there was considerable uniformity of opinion concerned the regulatory setup governing legal services and the role of the regulator. There was widespread dissatisfaction about the role of the regulator with regard to meeting the long-term needs and interests of the sector and with regard to its regulatory capacity, its competence, mandate, and representativeness. There were also concerns about inter-institutional coordination and the dynamics between the regulator and the line ministry. To a large extent, the arguments presented here are illustrative of the problem with self-regulation in professions, discussed earlier. The underlying concern is whether self-regulation and the monopoly that it gives with respect to entry and competition in India's legal services sector is necessarily conducive to ensuring quality and standards, to ensuring that regulations and capacity keep pace with the changing requirements of the profession and globalization, and to ensuring the larger interest as opposed to the regulator's self-interest.

Regulatory Setup and Representation Issues

It was pointed out by most respondents that the regulatory framework in legal services is weak. A primary reason for this weakness is due to the way in which the regulatory body is constituted, which according to almost all respondents is viewed as not sufficiently representing the emerging changes and future needs of this sector. A common view that emerged was the regulator primarily represents the interests of the litigation community as it consists mainly of members from the district court litigation and small firm segments, while the corporate advisory and LPO constituencies are unrepresented for the most part.[8] It was repeatedly stated that the regulator is more aligned with the representation side of the sector than with the transactional or advisory side of the segment. One respondent also noted that there is also a regional bias in its membership with a predominance of the Northern states.

The process by which members are elected is an area of concern for most legal professionals. The common perception is that the process is not sufficiently driven by the capabilities of the contesting candidates.[9] This feeling was expressed by many respondents, including lawyers working in both small and large firms, government officials, industry chamber representatives, and academics.[10] However, one positive development noted in this regard was that some corporate law firms are now putting their representatives on the regulator, which would enable better representation of the interests of the corporate segment in future.[11] It was also pointed out that there is very little informed debate or dissemination of information on issues such as reforms and opening up of the sector. As put by one respondent, "We need to get the right people on the regulator."

Another commonly voiced concern relates to the mindset and attitude of the regulator on issues such as marketing, solicitation,

---

[8] Big law firms are seen as having limited influence on the board.

[9] Being elected as a member of the BCI enables one to be a representative in the Bar Associations. Each state Bar Council sends one person to the BCI. The state Bar Council consists of around 35 members, but this number depends on the total number of lawyers in that state. The electoral roll is of the entire state. Most who contest the elections are district court lawyers involved in litigation and not high court lawyers. But often they may not be familiar with the rules and disciplines.

[10] Some respondents also stated that the elections are not clean. The majority consists of nonpracticing lawyers and many are not familiar with the disciplines and yet serve on the disciplinary body. The prevailing view is that the entire electoral process needs to be re-examined and the regulator needs to be reformed at the all India level with the inclusion of more ex officio members or members recommended by the judiciary to make it competent and credible body.

[11] The example of a partner from a leading Indian law firm who has recently become a member on the regulator was cited.

legal training and education, financing, and MDPs, which is an outcome of the aforementioned problems with the selection process. Several respondents pointed out that important functionaries of the regulatory body are often not active practitioners and are not conversant with the latest issues, such as what corporate advisory work entails or what corporate law firms do and about the latter's interests. In their view, even their concept of law and of law firms remains backdated. Law firms are seen as elitist by the regulator, according to most respondents. Hence, the regulator is seen as lacking initiative to address constraints (e.g., advertising and financing) which are hurting the competitiveness of Indian law firms and consequently, there is little interest on the part of forward looking, progressive practitioners to become members of the regulatory body, further compounding the problem of representation.

Another governance-related problem noted by many respondents is that of jurisdictional conflict between the regulator and the law ministry and problems of coordination between the two. It is widely felt that when the government has tried to bring change, it has not got the support of the regulator.[12] In general, stakeholders believe the ministry does not wish to take a lead role and in initiating required changes in the sector as it is unwilling to take a stand against the legal fraternity and prefers not to antagonize it for fear of flash strikes which would bring the courts to a halt. The lack of political will prevents any bold steps (such as required changes in the Advocates Act) from being taken in the sector and the status quo continues unlike the case in other countries where the government has often initiated changes to help strengthen the sector. It was also pointed out that the close nexus between politics and law is in part responsible for this lack of political will on the part of the government to change the status quo.

Hence, the regulatory setup is seen to have several shortcomings with regard to the process of representation, the capabilities and

---

[12] There have been conflicting positions on issues between the ministry and the regulator as evident from the affidavits filed by the two sides in the Bombay High Court Judgment with the former wanting reforms but the latter disapproving.

orientation of the regulator, conflicts of interest, and the power structure overseeing this sector, which in turn have a bearing on reforms and capacity building in this sector. According to respondents, such weaknesses in the regulatory setup make it difficult to have an informed discussion on important issues confronting the sector and to initiate required regulatory changes and capacity building measures. Such limitations in institutional capacity clearly underlie the lack of confidence in the regulatory setup that was expressed by most respondents.

Overall, the arguments relating to both the regulatory framework and the mandate indicate a problem endogenous to self-regulation of professions, which is the presence of vested self-interests which when combined with the ability to enforce this interest through the power of licensing and accreditation and erection of entry barriers, can result in adverse selection, the very information asymmetry that regulation in professional services is supposed to help overcome. The discussion on both these points also highlights the role of political will and the need to have the state as a more proactive player to co-regulate along with the professional regulator to curb such monopoly power and for the larger interest.

Regulatory Mandate

A related issue is that of mandate. Many stakeholders noted that the regulator in India has too wide a mandate. It is responsible for training, providing technical literature, conducting examinations, setting standards, accrediting institutes, disciplining, and governing, and helping the government in taking policy decisions. This is in contrast to the case of regulators in other countries who are primarily responsible for education and training while other functions are performed by sub-regulators or specialized bodies. Some respondents felt that having such a wide mandate prevents the regulator from performing its functions effectively and from keeping pace with developments and emerging requirements in the sector. According to many of them, the regulator lacks institutional capacity to handle such a gamut of functions. This limitation is most acutely felt by respondents in the area of standards and training. Many respondents feel that the present regulator is not the appropriate body for setting standards and licensing and that the Ministry of Human Resource and Development should take over the jurisdiction of exams and the accreditation of training institutions in this sector.[13]

The large mandate and the concentration of so many functions in one regulator are also seen as giving rise to conflicts of interest and creating a resistance to change, which is detrimental to the process of reforming the sector. For example, it was observed that it is difficult for the regulator to push through international standards or changes in legislation when the majority of its members are against such changes. Hence, it is difficult to maintain an arms-length principle across the different functions, even though, in principle, the various functions are independent of one another (regulation is technically independent of the training and development functions). Overall, it was felt that the self-regulation framework that is present in India is prone to conflicts of interest. But it should be noted that this debate is not unique to India.

Disciplinary Mechanisms and Scope

There was also considerable concern among many respondents about the regulator's ability to enforce discipline and handle violations of codes of conduct. Some very strong views were expressed in this regard, especially when compared with the record of other regulatory bodies such as the Institute of Chartered Accountants of India (ICAI). It was noted that the regulator may give notice in 10 out of 100 cases of violation but it is unlikely that the violator would be summoned. Penalties are rarely imposed, disciplinary proceedings are rarely held, and debarring is not common. In general, all respondents agreed that neither the litigation nor the corporate segment is sufficiently disciplined. Certain inherent limitations were also pointed out regarding the reach of the regulator's disciplinary mechanisms. For instance, only members can

---

[13] Interestingly, some respondents said that the sector is extensive enough to require sub-regulators.

be debarred from practice, but not firms as it is the professionals who sign the documents and are liable.

Other Issues and Concerns

The discussions also revealed the presence of several inherent structural and cultural factors that affect the global competitiveness of Indian law firms. Although some of these have already been highlighted in the course of the earlier discussion, they warrant separate mention as they have a bearing on the future of the sector and its ability to meet the competitive challenges ahead.

One key issue pointed out by respondents is that of a market structure. Many of those surveyed noted that the sector suffers from a major structural disadvantage, which is scale and fragmentation. More than 90 percent of Indian law firms are proprietary. There are very few large firms. Such firms cannot be expected to compete with foreign firms which have hundreds of partners and employee strength of several thousands. The small size of the majority of Indian law firms is in turn an impediment to the introduction of new systems and processes, business development, and thus competitiveness. Most respondents feel that without growth and consolidation Indian law firms will not be in a position to compete globally (though a small minority also believe that having many small firms, makes the market more competitive, as highlighted earlier). Further, with the emergence of corporate law divisions within companies and the opportunities in corporate law firms, looking ahead, the proprietary model of practice is expected to face problems of quality with the best law graduates moving into corporate practice or being picked up by foreign firms, as has been happening over the years. Hence, the very segment that is being protected today is declining in importance and this trend needs to be factored into prospective reforms and legislative changes, according to respondents.

Another inherent drawback of the sector that was repeatedly noted as affecting the growth of Indian firms is mindset and culture. As highlighted earlier, formation of LLPs and creation of larger firms, according to many practitioners, are being prevented by mindset, as proprietorship enables Indian lawyers to retain their autonomy and flexibility. It was mentioned that Indian firms do not have the mindset to work in partnership, to share profits, and share names. There is also reluctance to adopt modern practices and to upgrade their systems and offering of services. It is widely held that without a flexible mindset, without scale and upgrading of standards and services, without proper business models, and human resource management systems, Indian law firms will find it difficult to compete with the large foreign firms.

Concerns were also raised about the high cost of professional indemnity insurance which is needed to practice overseas. The maximum professional risk indemnity provided by Indian insurance is only around US$10 million while a typical foreign firm has over US$200 million in insurance cover. Premiums are very high internationally. One respondent mentioned that a firm could go bankrupt when getting indemnity insurance and only insurance on a transaction basis is possible. The lack of access to capital as highlighted earlier (due to unavailability of bank loans and reliance on retained earnings) compounds this problem. A minority of respondents, however, stated that professional indemnity insurance is not such a big issue nor is financing, and it is primarily mindset and lack of professionalism which makes the majority of Indian law firms uncompetitive.

Thus clearly, there are cultural and social dimensions to the competitive challenges faced by the Indian legal services sector. Some of the highlighted issues are also reflective of the level of development of the sector and the fragmented nature of the Indian legal services market in terms of both providers and clients for these services. Hence, the views expressed by the respondents are suggestive of the fact that regulatory reforms alone may not be sufficient for overcoming constraints to competitiveness. There may be a natural progression of a sector over a time as an economy evolves and with changes in cultural and social norms which can help address such challenges. The discussion also suggests that it is important to recognize the interplay of these various forces when designing regulation.

Views about Liberalizing Legal Services: Pros and Cons

The preceding discussion clearly highlights that there are numerous challenges, regulatory and otherwise which currently impede the competitiveness of Indian law firms and professionals. In the course of the in-depth discussions with legal professionals and industry experts it also became evident that many of these very constraints lie at the root of the concerns and sensitivities that mark the debate about the opening up of India's legal services sector to foreign firms, even if only in the corporate advisory segment. As highlighted earlier, FLFs are currently not allowed to practice either advisory or representational services in India. They operate through a fly-in-fly-out mode or by using third countries such as Singapore and Dubai for arbitration work or to fly out clients to these sites for providing advisory services.

Over the past decade or more, however, there has been much discussion about allowing FLFs to set up commercial presence in India and to practice in the corporate advisory segment, and the issue has evoked much controversy and debate among different sections of the Indian legal fraternity. There has also been pressure on the Indian government to open up its professional services sectors, including legal services in the context of the GATS negotiations in the WTO and in bilateral economic partnership and cooperation agreements.[14] Hence, although the primary focus of the discussions

---

[14] These include, for example, the India–EU broad-based Trade and Investment Agreement and the Australia–India Comprehensive Economic Cooperation Agreement, currently under negotiation. Under the GATS, an important recent development is the proposal for a plurilateral agreement on services. The US, the EU, and Australia along with some other like-minded members, called the Really Good Friends (RGF) of Services, have proposed a plurilateral approach to services negotiations that aims at significant opening up across sectors. This is generally known as The Trade in Services Agreement (TISA). The agreement is not yet signed but there is a growing pressure on India to be a part of this agreement. Participation in this agreement would mean additional pressure to provide market access in closed sectors such as legal services.

was to identify the constraints affecting India's legal services sector, an attempt was also made to elicit views on the pros and cons of opening up the sector and to understand how the various identified challenges and impediments impinge upon the prospects for liberalizing and reforming legal services in India.

When questions on these issues were posed to the stakeholders, as expected, there were strong and varying reactions. At one extreme there was complete opposition to the idea of FLFs in all forms and across all activities (including advisory services) in India on grounds of unfair competition, an uneven playing field and asymmetry in size and conditions. On the other extreme there was a strong pro-liberalization view advocating immediate opening up, based on the many benefits foreign firms could bring to the Indian legal sector, the existing operating frameworks and ground realities of the legal sector worldwide and the fact that India had already lost precious time by delaying liberalization. There was also a middle ground view endorsing gradual or limited opening up after a transition period, in recognition of potential benefits from tie-ups with foreign firms but subject to the fulfillment of certain conditions by other regulatory bodies and the implementation of interim measures in India, with impact assessment in the interim period to calibrate the liberalization process.

The views, however, could not be categorized by type of firm (i.e., by size, ownership/affiliation, family or nonfamily, etc.) as there was a mix of positions across different segments. However, regardless of size, affiliation, or ownership status, all firms expressed the need for regulatory reforms, including establishing a level playing field for Indian firms in the wake of eventual liberalization, removing some of the regulatory impediments to the operation of domestic firms, strengthening the sector and raising standards, and improving regulatory enforcement and capacity. Hence, as pointed out earlier, to a large extent, many of the issues that were raised when outlining the domestic regulatory constraints and competitive challenges in India's legal services sector were also used to justify the position taken on whether the sector should be opened up or not. The following discussion highlights first the arguments presented in opposition to opening up India's legal services sector followed by the arguments in favor of such liberalization, as noted by respondents.

Potential Adverse Implications of Opening Up

Many respondents expressed concerns about the likely adverse impact of opening up legal services on Indian firms and clients. They also questioned the purported benefits from such opening up. The views expressed were often quite extreme and even sensational in some respects, clearly reflecting a strong ideological opposition to opening up and no nuancing of issues.

Business-related Concerns

Most of the opposition to the entry of foreign firms in India, even in only limited segments is due to fears about loss of market share and business with clients and referrals going to foreign firms given their larger scale, deeper pockets and range of expertise. Several academics and experts who follow this sector noted that this concern is greatest among the top-end Indian law firms who fear an erosion of their current business from multinational corporations (MNCs) and large Indian clients. Some respondents went so far as to say that foreign firms would 'gobble up' the Indian firms by acquiring them or by squeezing them out of the market. They pointed out the likelihood of anticompetitive practices by foreign firms, including price undercutting in the initial stages to garner the domestic market. Examples were cited of such undercutting and it was pointed out that the foreign firms given their deep pockets, their scale and ability to cross subsidize, can afford such underpricing. Respondents said that even the premium domestic firms would not be able to sustain a low pricing strategy and would thus be competed out of the domestic market. Furthermore, the entry of foreign firms would only aggravate the existing competition to domestic firms, which has grown in recent years due to the growth in outsourcing and intense price competition from the large number of domestic players. Some respondents even stated that Indian firms are concerned about foreign firms not so much because they are afraid of competition or lack capabilities, but because of the financial strength of foreign firms. As regards loss of business, some said that the concern is not about losing Indian clients but about becoming the second choice for foreign clients and the latter can mean a significant loss of revenues.

There is also a concern that foreign firms would raise the cost of legal services in India (which probably presumes a predatory pricing strategy, whereby they would first undercut the Indian law firms and then raise their fees once they capture the domestic market). At present they are 3–6 times the cost of Indian firms and as foreign firms have standard international hourly rates, local clients would ultimately be forced to pay such high rates. Respondents cited the case of France and Germany where legal services had become costlier after foreign firms entered and domestic firms also raised their fees. The negative experience of English speaking, common law countries such as Australia and South Africa were also cited where foreign firms were seen to have squeezed out domestic firms from those markets. (It was mentioned that only one out of five big domestic firms had survived in South Africa within six months of entry by the foreign firms). It became evident during the discussions that such concerns about predatory pricing by foreign firms in part stems from the earlier discussions in the Joint Economic and Trade Committee (JETCO). These examples were given to emphasize the need to formulate a well thought out and calibrated strategy when allowing entry to foreign firms, rather than rushing into liberalization of the sector.

Although it is generally understood that FLFs would be interested in the legal advisory segment, several of those opposing their entry stated that there needs to be an assurance that the litigation segment will not be touched. The concern is that there would be a gradual encroachment into the domestic market, from the advisory to the representation segment. Several legal professionals who were interviewed noted that entry could move from business to advocacy, to litigation and representation in court, ultimately hurting the small law firms.[15] Moreover, once the larger firms are forced to cut rates to compete with the foreign firms, the smaller firms would be affected. So, even though the direct and immediate impact of foreign firms would be on the large Indian firms, it is feared that there would be a subsequent impact on all firms and on all segments in the sector.

Respondents also said that while Indian firms would lose their business to foreign firms, they would not be able to get more business from the foreign firms, thus losing both ways. In addition, the foreign firms would hire local lawyers and use local expertise and raise local costs. Some respondents went so far as to say that the entry of foreign firms could result in a monopolistic market structure with only a few big firms surviving, which would not be in the interests of Indian clients and the common man as the rates would rise by 4–6 times.

An important point made by several respondents was that India is the market that would face the most competition from foreign firms unlike other emerging markets such as China or Brazil. This is due to language and the compatibility of our common law system with that of countries whose firms are keen on expanding overseas. While China may have allowed FLFs to enter, language is a barrier and so our situation is not comparable to that of the Chinese and the likely adverse impact on domestic firms would be much greater than that seen in other emerging countries that have opened up this sector.

Concerns were also voiced about the possible ambiguities that could arise in the scope of practice for FLFs, if they are allowed to enter and to partner with domestic firms. For instance, would a JV with an Indian firm qualify a foreign partner to litigate? If foreign lawyers possess degrees which are recognized, then would they be allowed to practice in the representation segment? If foreign firms enter and have employees or partners with recognized degrees and

---

[15] It was pointed out that there have been representations from foreign legal delegations seeking access to Indian courts, thus indicating their interest beyond the advisory segment.

eligibility to litigate, then what would be the scope of their practice? At present only Indian nationals are allowed but under JVs and partnership formats, would practice depend on nationality or on qualifications? Thus, there is some concern that foreign lawyers could eventually end up going beyond advisory services and could compete in more areas with domestic lawyers. Such concerns again underscored the predominant view that any opening up of the sector has to be well thought through, and any such ambiguities regarding what the presence of foreign firms in the domestic market would entail, must be removed.

If one reflects on the gist of the issues highlighted above, it is that Indian firms would lose their clients and their livelihood to FLFs who would be able to undercut them or force them out of the market as they would be able to provide more services due to the scale and scope of their business, their brand name and their deep pockets. An assessment of the facts suggests that this argument may not be valid for the majority of Indian firms which are small proprietary concerns as the latter's client profile, fee structure, services, targets, and modes of operation are very different from those of foreign firms and also from their larger Indian counterparts. While the large majority of Indian lawyers charge nominal fees to their Indian clients, the big Indian law firms and leading lawyers charge very high fees which can only be afforded by big Indian businesses. Leading Indian lawyers are amongst the most highly paid professionals in India, charging five figure fees for a single appearance plus other perks and benefits from their clients. Top lawyers charge as much as ₹4 million (US$600,000) per appearance which can only be afforded by the leading Indian industrialists, the medium range charge around ₹1.5 million (US$20,000) per day while the more reasonable lawyers charge around ₹300,000–500,000 (US$5–8,000) per day (Iyer 2013; Sahgal and Bamzai 2010). According to some media sources, a one-man show by some leading Indian lawyers can result in billings of ₹400 million (US$6 million).

There is thus considerable segmentation in India's legal services sector and it is difficult to accept that the entry of foreign firms in the advisory and consulting segment would take away the business from the small Indian law firms given the strong divide between foreign and the small domestic firms. The threat to the survival of the small Indian law firms lies elsewhere has also became evident from the discussions. The real threat lies in the latter's old fashioned ways of practice and lack of growth opportunities given the limited range of services they offer, all of which are causing the best and the brightest law graduates in India to move into the legal cells of companies or to FLFs overseas as opposed to entering private practice. The threat of competition, however, appears to be much more justified in the case of the larger Indian firms in terms of their current business and their future growth prospects. This is the segment that is likely to overlap in terms of clients, fees, range of services, and strategies with the foreign firms. Apprehensions about being undercut by the foreign firms or use of influence by the parent company and use of brand name to get business may be valid for the larger Indian law firms, although to the extent that there is some competition for business between the small and large Indian firms, there may be an indirect impact on the small-scale segment as well. Overall, taking stock of the nature of the arguments presented on the loss of business loss following foreign entry, it appears that the interests of a few underlie the opposition to liberalization. But the argument is presented as representative of all segments of law firms. Much of this is conjectural and is difficult to substantiate without comparable evidence from other countries.

Employment-related Concerns

Another concern pertains to the employment implications of the entry of foreign firms. Several of those surveyed noted that domestic firms would lose out as foreign firms, which have attractive pay structures compared to domestic law firms, would employ local lawyers and divert the best employees by offering them much higher salaries which cannot be afforded by Indian firms. As a result, Indian firms would end up with lower quality lawyers or would need to match these salaries to retain their best employees, thereby raising their costs and eventually passing these costs on to Indian clients. Examples were given of other countries like

Singapore, where foreign firms have attracted the best professionals into their firms and have eventually been barred from employing local lawyers.

However, it is important to recognize that the views concerning employment displacement and skill clustering with the high-quality employees moving to the better paying, high-quality firms, including foreign firms and segmenting of the internal labor market are not unique to legal services. The creation of a dual labor market is an outcome that is commonly discussed in the literature on liberalization of professional services. It may even be characterized as one of the defining features of today's global economy. It is also important to note that such two-tiering of quality already exists in India's legal services sector, even without its liberalization, given the oligopolistic market structure. As already highlighted earlier, there are a few big Indian firms that hire the best and the brightest Indian law graduates and pay more attractive salaries than the majority of firms which are small and proprietary. American and British law firms are already recruiting Indian lawyers at the graduate level from premier law schools in India and employment diversion to overseas offices of foreign firms is already happening.[16] This, as pointed out by several respondents, has created problems of retention and has disincentivized firms from investing in training their employees though whether such competition for employees has led to an increase in wages is difficult to say in the absence of concrete information on employee costs. But to argue that liberalization would cause dualism in the labor market or the overall legal services market is to overemphasize the impact of opening up as such segmentation already exists.

It is possible, however, that liberalization and foreign competition could aggravate this dualism given the existing market structure in India's legal services sector and the asymmetries in size, scope, and other restrictions that put Indian law firms at a disadvantage

---

[16] On average 30 Indian students are recruited every year by the UK law firms. These graduates go through two years of training across various departments and then can practice English law by taking a qualifying exam.

vis-à-vis their foreign counterparts. Even the fact that a section of respondents feel that there are very bright, talented legal professionals in India who would be diverted to more competitive foreign firms alongside the argument that most of Indian legal education is not up to the mark, suggests that there is two-tiering within the legal education system as well. There is thus segmentation at various levels in India's legal services sector, in terms of organizations, fees, education and training, and clients. The question therefore is about who will be the most directly affected by the additional dualism that may arise from liberalization and whether there is a protectionist interest in advancing such arguments and couching these in the terminology of dualism. Once again, as with business concerns, much of the projected implications for the labor market following foreign entry remains conjectural and cannot be validated without hard facts and comparable evidence from other countries that have experienced liberalization in this sector.

Governance-related Concerns

There is also considerable concern among the Indian legal fraternity about the challenges that would be posed to regulators following foreign entry. One issue relates to the ambit of their regulatory powers, in particular, whether they also apply to LPO, fly-in-fly-out operations of foreign firms, and affiliations, and if so, to what extent and in what manner (as highlighted in an earlier chapter). The latter in turn raises concerns about the regulator's ability to monitor any indirect forms of operation by foreign firms. At present this is not possible as foreign firms are not recognized as legal entities in India.

Several respondents pointed to earlier violations of the scope of practice by some foreign firms (which had gone beyond collecting and giving market information to carrying out commercial activities in their view). The 'surrogate entry' of foreign firms through affiliates and liaison offices and the income tax tribunal cases against foreign firms were cited as evidence of the difficulties in governing foreign firms and their activities. There was a concern that if the sector were opened up, due diligence might not be done when allowing entry and that there would not be proper checks on the operations of foreign firms to ensure that, following their entry, they remain within the ambit of what is permitted under existing regulations. Respondents also highlighted the case of other countries such as Singapore which had opened up the legal sector only to experience malpractices by foreign firms, thus requiring them to change rules (e.g., requiring them to work with local firms, barring them from hiring local lawyers) to control such violations by foreign firms. Hence, there was considerable opposition to the entry of foreign firms on the grounds that there is limited ability to subject foreign firms to disciplinary action in India even if they are found to be violating existing codes of conduct. But as some respondents pointed out, there is an inherent contradiction in the current regulatory framework.[17] Unless foreign firms are allowed to establish themselves transparently as formal, recognized legal entities, how can they be subjected to the regulations and disciplinary mechanisms?

The case of the Indian legal services sector thus highlights an interesting point, that professional services may be caught between a situation of both over and under regulation. While one can argue that it would be in the self-interest of the regulator to actually over-regulate foreign firms to limit competition, the regulatory framework at least in the Indian context exhibits a contradiction in regulation. Foreign firms are not allowed to establish themselves, a feature that can be seen as an outcome of over-regulation of the market due to the presence of entry restrictions. At the same time, due to the presence of affiliate relationships with domestic firms, fly-in-fly-out and outsourcing arrangements, and lack of clarity about the legality of these other forms of presence, there

---

[17] Another ambiguity that was pointed out relates to tax procedures. Some foreign firms said that they need to be very careful to ensure that they are not present in India for more than three months in a financial year as otherwise they could be deemed to be a permanent establishment and become liable for taxes. It was noted that India is the only country where the substance becomes secondary to the process as foreign firms are constantly tracking the number of days their employees/partners have spent in India.

is in effect no appropriate regulation of these modes of operation. This illustrates the need to adapt regulatory frameworks and to upgrade regulatory capacity in line with changing market realities and forms of business.

Competitive Disadvantages and Uncertain Benefits

The issue of an uneven playing was cited by many respondents as a reason for delaying the entry of foreign firms. As Indian law firms suffer from many competitive disadvantages arising from the many structural and regulatory factors discussed earlier, many respondents felt that the sector should not be opened up till these constraints are addressed and Indian firms are placed on an even footing with foreign firms in terms of the scale and scope of their activities. For instance, only a handful of Indian firms have 100 plus lawyers. A quote from one of the respondents captures the essence of the uneven playing field argument with regard to size:

> How can we compete with these 2,000 member strong firms which have hundreds of partners while we have only single proprietary or very small partnership firms? They are very trained and specialized. There are very few Indian firms with 300 people. It is not fair to ask us to compete with such large firms. Under such a situation, why should we open up when Indian firms are subject to so many competitive disadvantages...?
>
> The problem with our market structure is that there are too many small firms and singleton lawyers sitting under trees and charging five rupees for preparing an affidavit....

In contrast, it was pointed out that foreign firms are not only large, but they also have a clear structure in place, possess knowledge databases, good management systems and information for handling all types of contracts and provide training for juniors. Small and medium size Indian firms cannot put in this kind of time and money.

In some areas, it was felt that the capabilities of our Indian law firms are still nascent and time needs to be given for the sector to mature and build capacity. Given the huge differences between Indian and foreign firms in terms of size, name, branding, finances, scope, experience, influence, contacts, etc. and the many restrictions which tie the hands of Indian firms, many respondents felt that it would not be fair to open up the sector to foreign firms without giving Indian firms a chance to prepare for this competition on a level playing field. These disadvantages would also prevent Indian firms from getting good work when they venture overseas as they lack size, marketing, brand and money power while foreign firms once allowed entry into the Indian market, would be able to garner the best work in India.

Thus, while opening up may potentially confer certain advantages, such as getting access to global markets and raising standards, the aforementioned competitive disadvantages must first be removed and the market needs to be given time to mature. The barrier between profession and business has to be broken. Restrictions on advertising and on the number of partners need to be removed. Policies need to be introduced to facilitate the access of Indian law firms to capital and to enable the formation of LLPs and steps need to be taken to develop capacity so that Indian firms are in a position to face competition from foreign firms as well as derive any associated benefits from greater international exposure and development of networks. Only then should the market be opened up. In general it was felt that our sector is not yet ready to internalize the potential benefits from opening up the sector.

There is also skepticism among sections of the legal fraternity about whether the purported benefits from opening up the legal services sector would actually accrue. As one respondent put it strongly, "Who needs them, the clients or the profession? The Indian legal profession is not for sale." It was mentioned that Indian industry is not demanding their presence and that it is the foreign firms which are seeking our market for new opportunities to make profits, as their own markets are saturated. Their sole interest, in this view, is to earn huge profits from doing business in India, saving on costs by hiring Indian lawyers to advise clients, and then repatriating these profits with little benefit to India. Hence, a question posed by some respondents is why Indian firms would want to share their business and revenues unless they are assured gains such as knowledge sharing and best practices? Respondents argued that foreign firms must show what benefits they will bring to Indian lawyers and law firms and that the real benefits would only accrue when foreign clients seek Indian law firms for their global strategies. The latter is not expected to happen in the near future according to many in the industry.

It was also pointed out that Indian clients do not stand to benefit in any major way from the entry of foreign firms as already they are accompanying their clients abroad and collaborating with foreign firms in overseas markets whenever local knowledge of those markets is required. When big Indian corporate groups are looking to invest overseas, they consult international law firms and while in India, they use Indian lawyers.[18] Due diligence in other jurisdictions is always done with the help of lawyers who have knowledge of local laws. The physical presence of FLFs in India is thus not required for this purpose as de-facto there is engagement of foreign lawyers. As a result, there is no major push coming from the corporate sector because consultation of FLFs is already taking place. Further, Indian law firms can also get access to information from foreign firms through their informal associations and networks, whenever required. So, one can argue that the physical commercial presence of foreign firms in the Indian market by changing FDI regulations in this sector is not essential to get these benefits.

Several respondents also questioned if the presence of foreign firms would increase employment opportunities for law graduates in India or lead to more outsourcing. This would require the total volume of business to increase, but the latter is not guaranteed as it depends on the state of the Indian economy and market conditions rather than the presence or absence of foreign firms. They further highlighted the fact that with the growth of corporate firms, MNCs and other businesses in India, there are already growing opportunities for Indian law graduates. Instead, it was argued, there would be increased repatriation of earnings from India. Hence, in their view, additional benefits with regard to employment that are often cited in favor of foreign firm entry, are likely to be small and

---

[18] An example was given where an Indian company was acquiring an oil refinery in Turkey and had to engage local lawyers.

tend to be overstated. Thus on balance, there is a risk that overall employment opportunities would not grow but there would be employment diversion from domestic firms and wages would rise due to poaching of the best lawyers by foreign firms and small firms in particular would not be able to retain their talent.

A small section of respondents also stated that as Indian lawyers are very good, there is no need to rely on foreign firms to help raise our standards. Indian law firms are catching up in specialized areas such as initial public offerings (IPOs), mergers, takeovers, etc.; they have become technology savvy and have access to modern databases and systems. Some have grown considerably and emerged as competent firms. As such changes are already happening without the presence of foreign firms, according to this view, there would be no special benefit from the latter's entry.

There was also a larger concern that opening up should be with a view to benefiting the larger legal system, not just the corporate segment and that the sector should not be viewed in silos. The real benefit to the common person would arise when the judicial system improves by bringing down the pendency of cases, by attracting better people into litigation, by upgrading, and modernizing through the use of technology and databases. But opponents of liberalization doubt that the entry of foreign firms would yield such benefits to the judicial system or to the common people.

Lack of Reciprocity

A common argument against opening up to foreign firms is the lack of effective reciprocal access for Indian law firms and legal professionals in other markets, a point also highlighted earlier. Indian law degrees are not recognized abroad and there is nothing in place for MRAs. This is seen as affecting the global competitiveness of Indian legal professionals. In addition, it was pointed out that Indian legal professionals face numerous other restrictions overseas, in the form of discretionary application of visa regulations (i.e., slow issuance of work visas, denial of visas even after getting sponsorship from a firm, and H1B restrictions), nationality and residency conditions and sub-federal restrictions in markets like the US where one needs to re-certify in order to practice across different states within the country. Even if they are able to practice in the EU or the US, they are not entitled to certain confidential documents to which the home country lawyer has access. Further, the scope of practice is limited for Indian lawyers. As one respondent put it, "There are many spokes in the wheel which deny recognition and subsequent entry and the first step is MRAs." Hence, there is also skepticism that even with MRAs, given the host of other conditions on entry and practice, effective access may be very limited.

In contrast, it was pointed out that foreign lawyers are able to operate in India in MNCs and in the legal wing of consulting firms and are not affected by such limitations. Once foreign lawyers enter India, they would be able to practice throughout the country while Indian lawyers would not be able to practice across different states in the US and would need to obtain state level permissions and licenses. A related concern is that once foreign firms enter India, they would get the business directly from Indian and foreign clients while Indian firms may not get the access to the overseas market or additional business. Hence, on grounds of lack of reciprocity, it was argued that since Indian lawyers are not provided opportunities to compete globally, unless they are given meaningful access to these markets, India should not permit foreign firms to practice in India.

There was, however, a counter view on reciprocity. Some respondents stated that this is not so important an issue but is often used to arouse apprehensions about the entry of foreign firms and thus to delay liberalization. Indian firms have opened offices in developed countries, Indian professionals have met the requalification requirements successfully and thus reciprocity is present and overseas markets are open. Indian lawyers work on corporate and commercial law and arbitration in the UK for instance and Indian lawyers can become partners in the UK as India is in the Foreign Registered Lawyers list of countries. Thus, in the view of this section of respondents, the reciprocity argument is not a valid one and the real concern of those who present this argument is to secure the Indian market for domestic firms. Further, they point out that there is limited interest among Indian firms in going abroad given their lack of finances and the high costs involved in setting up overseas operations. Moreover, certification is a requirement in this profession in all jurisdictions and is not a discriminatory practice that is specifically applicable to Indian lawyers. Even in the Indian market there are restrictions on foreign legal professionals through regulations on profit sharing, qualifications, and membership requirements. For instance, regulations do not permit Indian advocates to enter into profit sharing arrangements with persons other than Indian advocates. Membership with the BCI and a qualifying degree from a recognized institution in India are required for advising on domestic law. The recognition requirements are stringent even for Indian nationals holding a foreign degree as the foreign university must be recognized by the BCI and the concerned candidate must pass the BCI exam in substantive and procedural law subjects that are specifically needed to practice domestic law in India. Enlisting of a foreign university for the recognition of a degree obtained by an Indian national is subject to the approval of the Legal Education Committee of the BCI.

But how valid is a reason such as the lack of reciprocity as an argument against opening up? While reciprocity is in itself an important issue and MRAs need to be pursued, the lack of reciprocity argument seems to be overblown as a reason for denying market access to foreign firms and professionals. If indeed reciprocity in qualifications is important for leveling the playing field for Indian law firms, then why, till date, has the regulator not proactively sought the removal of various behind-the-border regulations or initiated MRAs with counterparts? Why has the legal fraternity at large not pushed the BCI more on this issue? Also, to the extent that many stakeholders feel that Indian firms are not that interested in setting up overseas (as noted by several respondents), how serious a problem is the lack of reciprocal access? These are some unanswered questions that warrant a rethinking on the strength of the reciprocity argument. Perhaps the issue of reciprocity is really a protectionist argument that is couched in a different terminology.

Is it being used to deflect attention from underlying problems of quality, competitiveness, and standards to prevent opening up of the sector? Some of the discussions on this subject certainly hint in that direction.

Views in Support of Opening Up

While many arguments were presented to support keeping the sector closed, there were also strong views expressed in favor of opening up the sector to foreign commercial presence through foreign equity participation or JVs and partnerships with local firms.[19] The reasons given included benefits in terms of standards, skills, employment, transfer of knowledge and best practices, infusion of capital, among others. This section of respondents also noted that to a large extent the legal community is misinformed about the intentions of foreign firms and the negative fallout of their entry. The point worth noting about the pro-liberalization arguments presented in this section is their direct contrast to some of the issues raised by those opposing liberalization and thus how opinion and ideology driven some of the arguments on both sides appear to be.

Benefits to the Domestic Market

One of the main benefits according to the proponents of opening up is that there would be *new and expanded opportunities* for associations and tie-ups for domestic firms, which would give rise to a variety of benefits such as access to other jurisdictions, access to databases and to specialized expertise, and to all the international offices of the foreign firm. Enhanced partnership opportunities and referrals made possible by foreign firms would in turn give rise to monetary and professional benefits, especially to the smaller Indian law firms. Opening up would also enable specialized training and upgrading of knowledge in emerging areas such as infrastructure

---

[19] According to the results of a recent Yougov survey, 96 percent of respondents support the liberalization of India's legal services sector, with 79 percent supporting full liberalization, i.e., practice of foreign and Indian law and 60 percent saying that opening up should happen within the next two years. But the objectivity of this survey and selection of respondents was questioned.

financing, energy, PPP, IPR, etc. In this regard, it was also mentioned that the presence of foreign firms would enable domestic clients to get expertise in these specialized areas. Such expertise is very limited in supply in the domestic market while there is a pressing need for specialized knowledge in these areas, given the needs of the Indian economy.[20] Indian companies need legal advice on large infrastructure projects and need products and solutions from lawyers, but our lawyers are not able to provide such expertise. Magic and Silver circle firms would provide opportunities to Indian professionals to train and to get exposure to international work.[21]

On the business front, those who support the opening up of the sector believe the entry of foreign firms would help expand the volume of business and increase the viability of Indian law firms. It would also benefit the sector as a whole, directly and indirectly. Transaction work and international arbitrations which are currently being done overseas would instead get done in India, thereby expanding business opportunities in India. Increased competition from foreign firms would also help lower costs for Indian businesses, thus benefiting their bottom-line while at the same time providing them with greater expertise. The litigation community would also benefit from the increased volume of transactions on the corporate law side and at the same time, they would not face any direct threat. There would be increased opportunities for LPOs in India. In addition, the exposure provided to legal professionals by the internationalization of the sector would yield benefits to our judicial administration system through the adoption of best practices, knowledge sharing, and reduced pendency

---

[20] One respondent stated that we need about US$1 trillion in infrastructure financing for which lawyers specialized in this area are needed. But India has only some 50 domestic lawyers with expertise in infrastructure. So, we need foreign legal expertise due to lack of domestic supply.

[21] The Magic circle is an informal term for the five leading law firms headquartered in the UK and the four or five leading London-based commercial barristers' chambers. The Silver circle is a group of corporate law firms headquartered in London, which have much lower turnover than the Magic circle firms but significantly higher profits and revenue than the national average.

of cases and appointments. It is also felt that increased international exposure could also help influence the strategies and aspirations of Indian law firms, motivating them to go abroad to other English-speaking countries with the common law system.[22] It could also help India become an arbitration hub for settling inter-country disputes.

To validate these gains, examples were cited about the gains realized by markets such as Germany, Japan, and Singapore following liberalization of their legal services sectors. The evidence shows that the growth in the number of lawyers increased post-liberalization (was 50 percent higher), new jobs were created in the sector, and the work that had been done abroad previously was brought back to those countries.

With the entry of foreign firms and partnerships with Indian law firms becoming possible, there was the potential for *financial gains* due to increased fees. At present, Indian firms take advance fees and get a portion from foreign firms, around 2 to 5 percent, in the form of a retainer fee. Once formal partnerships and fee sharing are permitted, Indian firms would be able to get a larger share. Many Indian firms get a large part of their work through referrals from FLFs. Formal partnership arrangements would enable Indian firms to better leverage such opportunities and to overcome the limitations they currently face under Best Friends and other networking arrangements (as in the latter cases, they are forced to join hands with only one firm). Hence, they can derive more benefits with formal opening up of the legal sector as opposed to the current alliances with foreign firms which are not formally recognized.[23] Moreover, if sharing of profits is permitted with best friends and sharing of

---

[22] Several respondents mentioned that Indian law firms are not really strategizing with business and growth targets. Their work is mainly to facilitate their own profile but they are not looking at new markets and domains.

[23] Although many respondents believe networks and alliances are useful (citing the case of some firms which have used these tie-ups to grow and gain visibility), it was repeatedly pointed out that such alliances suffer from limitations of exclusivity in referrals and possible conflicts of interest. Hence, many of these best friends' relations have fallen apart. It is believed that allowing formal partnerships and profit sharing with foreign firms would yield greater benefit in terms of transfer of know-how, access to training, improved finances, and access to global networks.

profits with non-advocates is permitted, then it could also help address the financing constraints currently faced by domestic law firms. More formal arrangements would also help foreign firms as the current ambiguities about tax liabilities under fly-in-fly-out operations would be removed.[24]

Growth in business is also expected to help *increase employment opportunities* for domestic lawyers. In addition, as the majority of staff in the foreign offices of law firms tends to be from the host country, Indian lawyers stand to gain from the entry of foreign firms. This is because the FLFs are interested in hiring quality Indian lawyers. At present, there is a lack of good professional opportunities in India's corporate law segment as domestic firms are not able to absorb the growing numbers of law graduates and to meet their aspirations in terms of salaries and career path. This is causing us to lose our bright, young lawyers who are currently getting recruited by foreign firms directly from reputed law schools or from the domestic law firms.[25] Indian law firms are having difficulties in retaining talent in India. The attrition rate is as high as 60 to 65 percent for the large firms and without the necessary investment in training and career progression, young Indian lawyers will continue to go abroad to join foreign firms. The junior partners are not fully trained and lack experience. There is also a lack of opportunities for internships for law students. As one proponent of liberalization puts it, "We have lost decades in capacity building and a pool of professionals due to rising attrition rates. Our young professionals are going to foreign firms." Hence, according

---

[24] Foreign respondents mentioned that if under fly-in-fly out arrangements a firm has spent more than 90 days in India, it is seen as a permanent establishment making it liable for withholding tax and corporate profit tax. The Indian tax authorities apply these rules at their discretion.

[25] This was corroborated by one of the respondents from a UK law firm who stated that they have been recruiting Indian lawyers at the graduate level from the premier schools in Bangalore, Hyderabad, Jodhpur, and Kolkata for the past seven years or so, and on an average 30 students are recruited every year. These graduates go through two years of training on a rotation basis in various departments of the firm, like English lawyers and then can practice English law by taking the QLTT exam.

Political Economy of Liberalization

to this view, the presence of foreign firms in the corporate advisory segment would enable us to retain and attract back talent, which would be beneficial for the sector as a whole.

It was also felt that the professionalism of foreign firms, once they are allowed to enter the Indian market, would help address the family-dominated structure that currently exists in India's law firms, where only family members can become partners, and thus enable the *internationalization* of Indian firms. FLFs, according to the proponents would help Indian law firms in becoming more global in their mindset, their work, their standards and practices and would also encourage Indian firms to go overseas and enter into partnerships and mergers and acquisitions. Indian firms would be more likely to enter into partnerships and to expand their scale of operations following the entry of foreign firms.

The entry of foreign firms is also expected to *benefit clients*, especially those operating across different jurisdictions as the law firms would then be able to provide seamless services to their clients. Many of the services currently done abroad would be done in India. This would enable the firms to control the quality of their services and to retain their clients across jurisdictions as they would not need to rely on fly-in-fly-out operations (which involve transactions costs and can run into ambiguities on the tax front). The legal sector would be able to play its role as a business enabler more effectively if the sector is opened up.

Formal recognition of FLFs in the country would also help improve *governance*. As one respondent put it,

> At present, they are in dark, smoky rooms. The advantages of getting them out into the light would be that we can hold them accountable. We have professional negligence rules, professional liability rules, conflict rules, privilege rule, which will then apply to the foreign firms. If they are sitting in some other place and flying-in and flying-out, that accountability does not exist. So, whether it is us as Indian lawyers who have to interact with our foreign counterparts or whether it is the Indian business or client who has to, it just makes more sense to have them accountable if they are already here.

Overall, supporters of liberalization feel that Indian firms would become stronger, would be able to provide a wider range of services and their quality would improve with the opening up of the sector. The entry of foreign firms is also expected to force a re-think on regulations and regulatory frameworks and enable a better understanding of best practices in other jurisdictions which may then be adopted in India, benefiting Indian law firms.

It is also important to consider the validity of the arguments presented in favor of opening up. Will the benefits in terms of standards, practices, employment opportunities, better services for Indian clients really materialize? It is difficult to answer this question based on the available evidence. There is only limited evidence to suggest that firms which have entered into affiliations with foreign firms (through Best Friends Relations for instance) have reaped benefits in terms of growth and enhanced capacity. This is because most of these relations have broken and many Indian firms have chosen not to enter into such tie-ups. So, it is hard to say if formal arrangements with foreign firms such as through partnerships or JVs, if these were allowed, would necessarily benefit Indian firms.

The positive fallout indicated for employment is not easy to validate either as this would depend on the growth of overall business opportunities, which is more a function of how the Indian economy performs, the growth of client firms, and the resulting demand for legal services by these clients. It may have less to do with the entry of FLFs or the presence of affiliated Indian firms. If the overall pie does not expand significantly, then the outcome could be in terms of redistribution of the available business and the jobs. However, to the extent that a wider range of services might be available through the foreign firms and their affiliates, there could be benefits to Indian clients and spillover effects on the rest of the sector through learning and competition. One can conclude that ultimately, the projected benefits from foreign firm presence in terms of improved standards, skills, nature of work, etc., would depend on the ability of Indian legal practitioners and firms to internalize these spillovers, in the absence of which there can be adverse effects from increased competition and diversion of talent.

Misplaced Fears and Misperceptions

It was also pointed out by many respondents that there is a lot of misunderstanding about what the entry of foreign firms would entail and what foreign firms are interested in practicing in India. The argument is that there are misplaced fears and perceptions created by some firms and by the regulator that foreign firms would enter into representation and litigation services and take away business of the small firms and the litigating lawyers. But the reality is that foreign firms are interested only in corporate advisory services for Indian clients looking at overseas markets or for foreign businesses looking at the Indian market. Hence, they would be in direct competition only with the larger Indian firms and not the smaller firms or the litigating lawyers. Foreign firms are not interested in practicing in our courts, but a different perception has been created to stir opposition to the very idea of allowing foreign firms to enter India even in the advisory segment.

It was also pointed out that the perception of competition is much bigger than in reality as the number of firms who would like to set up office in India is not that large. Such presence is also nothing particular to India as law firms routinely set up international offices in other countries and hire local lawyers to advise their clients in other jurisdictions. Hence, there is no particular malintention of foreign firms with respect to the Indian market as this is not a new phenomenon in the legal sector. Moreover, unlike in the accountancy sector, law firms do not have the same kind of brand name and presence and so concerns about their entry are overblown. Reputed and competent Indian law firms would continue to be important and client relationships would continue to be maintained.

Some respondents also stated that Indian law firms are competent and thus need not fear foreign firms. In this context, they pointed out the sector is in many ways already open through the fly-in-fly-out route and there is already a fair degree of foreign competition but Indian firms are faring well. For instance, FLFs based out of other countries like Singapore and Hong Kong have Indian lawyers who come to India regularly and do the work in

India like FLCs. Indian firms should therefore not feel threatened by the commercial presence of foreign firms.

On similar lines it was also argued that as knowledge of local laws and the role of jurisdiction are very important in law, there is less to fear from foreign competition than in sectors such as accountancy services where practices are much more globally standardized. In the case of law, automatic protection is provided by national boundaries and local knowledge. In addition, conditions such as nationality requirements would automatically limit the foreign firm's ability to practice in the domestic market. Respondents also noted that opening up could be done in a calibrated and phased manner and conditions pertaining to employment, scope of practice, number of licenses, etc. could also be imposed to allay concerns about loss of business, diversion of employees, and other such adverse impacts on domestic firms, along the lines of the various "behind-the-border regulations" which affect our professionals overseas.[26]

Another important point that was highlighted is that Indian clients are already sending out their work to London, Dubai, and Singapore where Indian and foreign lawyers are advising Indian or foreign client firms and arbitration is also being done in other jurisdictions. With the presence of foreign firms, work that is currently going out of the country would instead get done in India and this would be beneficial to Indian law firms and Indian clients as it would reduce their transaction costs. Contrary to the perception that good legal professionals would join FLFs following the latter's entry the reality is that many good Indian legal professionals are already leaving the country and joining FLFs overseas.

---

[26] An interesting point was made in this context regarding reciprocal access. Several respondents who support opening up said that little is being done to enter into MRAs. In their view, this issue is being used as a convenient argument to prevent opening up as the primary interest is in securing the market here rather than in getting access overseas. It was pointed out that these very lawyers who advocate the opening up of other sectors, as it creates opportunities for them, oppose the liberalization of their own sector. Thus, it is perceived by some that those opposing liberalization are doing so only for vested interests or on ideological grounds and not on a sound economic basis.

By opening up, we would be able to retain these professionals in the country. It was further pointed out that with the advent of the Internet and the reduced cost of bandwidth, legal services will increasingly get stratified between routine and elite legal services and jurisdiction and geography may diminish in importance. In light of such trends, it would be important to internationalize to take advantage of these new trends and opportunities.

The issue of reciprocity was also raised as one that has been misunderstood and misrepresented. According to one foreign legal professional, the UK legal services market is open and many FLFs including some Indian firms are practicing there. Foreign lawyers are permitted to practice English law, subject to qualifying in an exam. They are allowed to practice foreign law in the UK. Hence, Indian lawyers and firms have access to the UK market and there is no discriminatory treatment. Indian lawyers can give legal advice barring in certain areas (transfer of real estate, practice in courts, wills) and can use the title of solicitor or barrister.

Thus, according to the proponents of liberalizing legal services, concerns about foreign competition are exaggerated, in part due to lack of an informed understanding about the issues involved. The concerns voiced by those opposing the presence of foreign firms and arguments based on level playing field and time needed to equip the sector are seen as ill-founded and as arguments of convenience to thwart foreign entry. As one respondent put it, "How much more time do we need? Two decades is too long in the business and we are ending up losing a generation of professionals. We have grown from 30 to 400 in 85 years, then how can we compete internationally?"

Reflecting on the Findings

The survey findings highlight a wide range of issues and challenges, some inherent, some policy-induced, that are relevant to the debate on liberalizing and reforming legal services in India. These include issues of market structure, regulatory setup, legislation, governance, training and standards, ethics and reciprocity, among others. On several issues, the arguments are similar to that found in the general literature on the regulation of professional services and also mirror discussions that have characterized this sector in other countries that have debated and undergone regulatory reforms and liberalization of their legal services sectors. The fraternity is, however, clearly divided on whether liberalization of India's legal services sector is desirable at least at this stage and whether at all it would be beneficial for firms and professionals in the sector. The arguments presented reflect differing perceptions and attitudes about the needs, objectives, and future path of this sector, to a great extent colored by the respective positions and interests (defensive or offensive) of the respondents. There is, however, one common underlying thread to the discussions, i.e., that outdated regulations are holding back the competitiveness of Indian law firms and professionals and that regulatory reforms are needed, whether or not opening up takes place, if the sector is to keep pace with global trends and opportunities. The discussions also clearly highlight the interdependent nature of the debate on regulatory reforms and liberalization in India's legal services.

Inconsistencies in Views and Arguments

Although it is difficult to assess the validity of the various views expressed given the lack of hard evidence and the conjectural nature of many of the points made, one aspect is worth highlighting. This relates to the often inconsistent nature of the arguments presented on certain issues, especially with regard to the adverse consequences of liberalizing legal services. These inconsistencies raise doubts about the validity of some of the positions expressed by the opponents of liberalization and whether the arguments are largely opinion-based or have some grounding in reality.

Take for instance the issue of costs of legal advisory services. While those opposing the entry of foreign firms argued that the latter would engage in anticompetitive practices and would undercut to take away business from domestic firms, this same section of respondents also argued that entry of foreign firms would lead to higher fees for legal services and increased costs for Indian clients, thus hurting the common consumers. Such a dual position on the issue of fees and costs can only hold if the underlying premise is that entry by foreign firms would result in predatory pricing by the latter, with prices being undercut initially followed by higher fees once the Indian firms have been outcompeted in the domestic market. Further, such a premise would require significant ability on the part of FLFs to take away long-established business from domestic law firms only on the basis of prices, notwithstanding any initial disadvantages they may have in terms of lack of familiarity with local laws and requirements, which according to some of these same respondents is difficult as legal services are a highly customized and jurisdiction-dependent activity, where relationships and networks are important. Hence, there was lack of articulation on the dynamics of prices, services, customer segments, etc. and the process by which such outcomes would be felt in the Indian market and the assumptions underlying these potential effects contradicted other common assumptions and arguments.

Likewise, it was argued that there is limited paying capacity among Indian clients but at the same time there were concerns that Indian clients would shift to foreign firms and pay higher fees. Even if the latter was true, there was no clarity on how big is the client segment with paying capacity that can be diverted to FLFs and further how much of a dent foreign firms would make in the market share and profitability of domestic firms due to such diversion of business? If this is indeed not too big a segment of the client market, then how serious is the threat of losing business to foreign firms? No hard facts and figures were provided to help validate this concern.

On the issue of alliances and networks, again contradictory views emerge from the same section of respondents. Opponents of liberalization argue on one hand that such arrangements are yielding benefits to Indian firms but it is not clear why the formal commercial presence of these same foreign firms and partnerships with Indian firms would not yield the same or greater benefits? Also, while some of these opponents argue that domestic firms are not equipped to internalize the benefits of foreign commercial presence and thus need time to prepare for foreign competition, it is also argued that there is no need for foreign competition as Indian firms are very capable and competent. Thus, the significance of such networks and alliances and the current capacity and maturity of the sector is unclear and both sides of the same issue are presented.

Similarly, with regard to the question of reciprocal market access, there is a lack of consistency in the arguments. While lack of reciprocity is often given as a reason for not allowing entry to FLFs, the same section of respondents also argue that Indian law firms are not that interested in going overseas due to the high costs involved and because the domestic market is lucrative enough. Therefore, some respondents believe that it is not important to grant access to foreign firms in our market to enhance access for Indian firms overseas as such access is not so important for our firms. Given these contradictions the significance of "lack of reciprocity" as a reason for denying entry to FLFs remains unclear.

With respect to employment opportunities, the arguments presented are again often inconsistent. Opponents of liberalization state that the entry of foreign firms will cause law graduates to move from the Indian firms given the former's higher salary structures and opportunities for career advancement. However, this same section also argues that there are ample employment opportunities being provided by Indian law firms and by the corporate law sector and thus no major benefit to be derived by Indian legal professionals from the entry of foreign firms. If there are indeed growing business and employment opportunities, then why is there so much concern about the possible diversion of employees to foreign firms?

Thus, many of the reasons provided for opposing the entry of FLFs can be questioned and seem to lack sound basis. Notwithstanding such inconsistencies and contradictions in views, however, it is quite evident from the range of concerns expressed and the range of benefits foreseen that this subject is a sensitive one. It is also interesting to note that there is no clear division among firms in terms of who represents which point of view. Respondents from both large and small firms oppose liberalization but there are also some large and small firms which support liberalization. This lack of a clear divide indicates that the views are shaped by perceptions and awareness and by the particular circumstances, objectives, and outlook of individual respondents and not necessarily hard evidence that can be substantiated with facts and figures.

Validity of Certain Concerns and Arguments

In addition to the apparent contradictions in several arguments that are common to the debate on liberalizing legal services in India, there are also apparent discrepancies between some of the issues and competitive challenges highlighted as reasons for opposing liberalization. There are also arguments which need to be analyzed more closely as they appear to represent the views of certain sections of the legal community, though these are often presented as reflecting the views of the entire profession. Such discrepancies again cast doubt on the validity of the arguments made against liberalizing legal services and also the motivation underlying them.

Take for instance one of the most commonly cited reasons for opposing liberalization, i.e., the lack of an even playing field for Indian professionals and firms as regulations prevent Indian law firms from scaling up by increasing the number of partners, from expanding the scope of their services to cover multiple disciplines, and from marketing themselves, thus putting them at a disadvantage vis-à-vis foreign firms. But as the preceding sections have shown and noted, these constraints are not binding. For instance, although the regulation on firm size allowed up to a maximum of 20 partners before the enactment of the Companies Act, 2013, for the most part, Indian law firms remained much smaller and many were single-owner proprietary firms, much smaller than the permitted maximum. Hence, the ceiling on size is clearly not as critical a regulatory impediment as is often projected. Also, as noted already, the small scale and fragmented nature of India's legal sector is more a fallout of other factors such as mindset, financial constraints, difficulty in building partnerships, etc. This is not to say that the restriction on size is justified, but it would appear that the repeated use of this argument as a constraint to growth and against the opening up of the sector may not be justified given the existing market structure and firms' preference toward staying small.

Likewise, one needs to objectively analyze the extent to which restrictions on soliciting and advertising put Indian firms at a competitive disadvantage and provide a basis to oppose the entry of foreign firms. Clearly, this is a profession where trust, reputation, references matter more than marketing for securing clients. It is also not clear to what extent a small proprietary firm would be able to overcome their size and other basic disadvantages vis-à-vis FLFs even if they were able to advertise, given the huge asymmetries that exist between these two kinds of firms. There is also evidence to suggest that this restriction is not monitored that closely in India and with recent relaxations on advertising and use of the Internet, this may be less of an issue today. Thus, this too does not seem to create as critical a disadvantage for Indian law firms as is often projected. Again, this is not to justify the presence of such a restriction and there is merit to the argument that it should be removed as it does not reflect the current practice on advertising in other countries.

Some Points of Convergence

There are, however, some issues where there is uniformity of opinion across all players in the sector and some clear conclusions that can be drawn. One such issue concerns the regulator and the regulatory structure in this sector. As discussed earlier, respondents find many shortcomings in the current setup, including lack of representativeness, conflicts of interest, difficulties with enforcing codes of conduct and education and training standards, etc.

An assessment of the current constitution of the regulatory body suggests that there is an inherent conflict of interest in terms of the wide mandate, and that there is lack of clarity about who holds precedence, the regulator or the line Ministry. On key issues where reforms are needed or a re-thinking is required, jurisdictional conflicts appear to be preventing initiatives from being taken. There seems to be some basis to the argument that short-run considerations are driving policies in the sector appears to be correct, and greater political will and far-sightedness are required.

Similarly, views expressed regarding preparedness and capacity and enforcement of standards of training and education also seem to have basis. In fact these views on training and standards are consistent with the Vision Statement 2010–2012 of the chairman of the BCI which highlights the required direction of legal education reforms in India and the associated steps.[27] The statement explicitly identifies two main weaknesses in the Indian legal education system; first, the inadequate quality of legal education and infrastructure, and second, the lack of relevant skills training to meet changing requirements In this note, the BCI states that Indian legal education must not only aim at creating value for the "top of the pyramid law graduates but must have stringent minimum standards for all law students…" with the objective of putting in place required measures from the 2011–2012 academic year. The steps identified in this statement include creating clear quality standards for legal education and a common entry level standard for admission to law schools nationwide, which would be made possible through a combination of institutional reforms aimed at quality control, benchmarking and accreditation processes; changes in the content and structure through revisions in the curriculum and more practical orientation; and improvements in pedagogy through the use of new technologies and mediums, faculty upgrading and incentives, among other measures.

Hence, there are evident problems with accreditation, the quality of training, and availability of specialized legal expertise. The absence of mechanisms to ensure upgrading of skills and knowledge and re-certification (till recently) and the lack of modern practices as well as the lack of investment in management systems and in-house training at the firm level also emerge as important shortcomings. The heightened awareness in policy circles regarding these latter limitations only confirms this fact and the broad

---

[27] See http://www.barcouncilofindia.org/bar-council-announces-proposed-directions-for-reform-in-legal-education/ (last accessed on January 1, 2015).

consonance between the survey findings and current thinking on these issues highlights the importance of capacity building and quality upgradation in this sector.

Another shortcoming that emerges in the regulatory framework is the lack of clarity and the absence of a coordinated and integrated approach to introducing new legislations and amendments. While LLPs are allowed, without associated amendments in the Advocates Act and without clarity on related issues such as taxes and scope of operations, this format cannot take off in the legal sector.

The approach to governance is also problematic as the regulator does not recognize FLFs formally and there remains ambiguity about what constitutes foreign legal practice (i.e., whether this includes LPOs, fly-in-fly-out operations, affiliate firms and such formats). Yet, without this clarity, it is not possible to regulate the FLFs' operations and circumscribe their activities. (The Bombay and Madras High Court cases reflect this ambiguity on definitions and scope of what foreign presence means, though these courts have clarified what legal practice includes in India.)

As regards regulatory restrictions on the operations of firms, while the implications of restrictions on advertising, scale and scope are ambiguous for the various reasons highlighted earlier, the implications of the restrictions on alliances and networks seem less ambiguous. The survey findings suggest that these restrictions do have an adverse effect on Indian firms. Indian law firms which have formed Best Friends Relations with FLFs and would like to reap the associated advantages of visibility and branding are unable to show their affiliation formally. This creates an undesirable situation where firms wish to benefit from international networks and tie-ups, but cannot do so openly, leading to concerns about surrogate presence of the foreign firms and back-door entry and difficulties in monitoring their activities. The restriction seems misplaced on two counts. First, it fails to recognize the way in which law firms tend to operate internationally. Second, it creates problems of governance. It would be far more effective to allow such affiliate firms to operate in a transparent manner and to bring them and their "friend" firms under the ambit of the regulator's disciplinary mechanisms. This would not only serve the interests of the medium and large Indian firms who wish to modernize and become more globally networked, but also enable the governance of all firms in the sector on an even footing, under the existing disciplinary mechanisms.

Key Takeaways

Overall, the survey findings and their analysis suggest that the root problem in India's legal sector seems to lie in the regulatory setup. Many of the issues that have been raised, such as problems of governance, lack of preparedness, problems with the quality of legal education and training, and failure to take an independent, long-term view of the legislative and regulatory requirements in the sector are due to weaknesses in the regulatory and institutional structure, in particular, its constitution, the wide mandate given to a single professional body and ambiguities about the relationship between the regulator and the state. If one were to prioritize among the issues and concerns raised, the regulatory environment and training and capacity building issues are perhaps the most important areas to be addressed in India's legal sector.

The analysis also indicates that much of the debate surrounding the issue of opening up of legal services in India is driven by specific interests and the political economy of the sector. Further, the debate has often been couched in arguments of convenience, possibly to divert focus from measures that need to be undertaken by the regulator and by the domestic firms. Cross-country evidence on regulatory practices reveals that there is ample scope to limit the operations of FLFs to allay concerns with respect to employment, business, conduct, and costs and that a gradual and circumscribed approach to liberalization is the norm. Hence, the strong views often expressed in India about the possible adverse consequences of FLFs may not always be that well founded as there are many ways in which domestic interests can be safeguarded. It is for the domestic regulator to safeguard these interests by inscribing appropriate conditions and limitations on foreign firms without thwarting competition. Perhaps this confidence in regulatory capability is lacking among domestic stakeholders. Overall, there appears to be a combination of both a misunderstanding and a possible misrepresentation of the issues by certain sections of the legal sector in India. Finally, there is the classic problem that characterizes the process of reforms in any sector, i.e., the incumbency problem, where the onus of initiating and implementing reforms lies with the incumbent regulator, resulting in a conflict of interest and resistance to change.

6
A Roadmap for Reforms

The overview of the legal services sector in the global and Indian contexts and the analysis of the available primary and secondary evidence provide broad directions for the policy reforms and measures that are needed if India's legal sector is to be strengthened. Clearly as the analysis in the previous chapter has highlighted, these measures must aim at addressing the shortcomings in the regulatory structure, at alleviating some of the constraints to the growth of Indian firms that arise from outdated and ineffective regulations, enhancing capacity and standards and encouraging a more global outlook and mindset. It is important to recognize that these actions are not contingent on the liberalization of the sector. Irrespective of whether this profession is opened to foreign firms or not, there are inherent weaknesses and regulatory gaps that need to be addressed in the long-term interests of the sector. They are needed for the overall growth and competitiveness of the sector and to prepare it for emerging challenges and opportunities in the future. Furthermore, with the progressive liberalization of the Indian economy, these reforms and measures become all the more important if the sector is to keep pace and to serve the interests of the Indian economy and Indian businesses.

Several initiatives can help strengthen this sector. These can be classified as broad initiatives in terms of defining an overall approach and strategy for reforms and capacity building in this sector, and targeted initiatives in terms of addressing specific issues or legislations.

Broad Initiatives

First and foremost is the need for dialogue and more informed discussion among all stakeholders, namely, the government, the regulatory body, the law firms (large, small, and medium, foreign), and the clients. The study indicates that there is a disconnect among stakeholders and that often times the issues and concerns are misplaced, not well understood, or given undue importance, in part due to a lack of discussion across different sections of the profession. In part this lack of open exchange results from lack of will among some sections, including the regulator to change the status quo and to address their own inadequacies. More dialogue in open forums representing all interest groups would facilitate an understanding of each other's perspectives and could address some of the concerns, thus facilitating reforms and introduction of new measures. The government, through the Ministry of Law and Justice is probably the best placed to take this initiative. It could hold periodic stakeholder consultations on specific issues, such as required amendments in the Advocates Act, the implications of LLP, reciprocity, domestic regulations affecting Indian law firms, etc., so that the decision-making process is more consultative and representative than appears to be the case at present.

Related to the need to promote exchange of views is the need to educate stakeholders. Very often, stakeholders have their own perceptions of issues but such perceptions are not necessarily well-informed. For instance, the discussions and roundtables revealed that reforms are automatically equated with opening up of the sector by some stakeholders and that the issue of reforms and capacity building is often not seen as an independent issue. There is also lack of clarity among various stakeholders about what exactly opening up and reforms mean in this sector. Due to the lack of awareness and sensitization, there is a general resistance to change and there are strong positions driven by biases as opposed to reasoned understanding. Thus, sustained efforts by the government and by the regulatory bodies as well as independent legal experts and academics are needed to promote informed debate and to address mindset and attitudinal factors which are holding back reforms.

Most importantly, there is a need for a long-term approach. The reforms should not be guided by short-term advantages or disadvantages; rather they should cater to the needs of the profession in the coming years. With an increasingly liberalized Indian economy and growing demands by other countries to open up professional services, such a long-term outlook with short- and medium-term action plans, becomes all the more important. Unfortunately, the current orientation in this sector appears to be driven by short-term, sectional interests and political economy dynamics compounded by a lack of political will to initiate required changes in legislation and regulatory oversight.

Targeted Measures

Analysis of the available primary and secondary evidence in this sector suggests three specific but interdependent areas where measures are needed. The first pertains to reforming the regulatory structure. The second pertains to strengthening governance in the sector. The third involves preparing the domestic sector for the future by removing constraints and developing domestic capacity through specific initiatives.

Regulatory Structure

The current regulatory framework in terms of assignment of responsibilities and ability to regulate needs a rethink in India. There seems to be a need to disperse some of the functions currently under the regulator so that it can perform its duties more effectively. The functions of enforcing standards, codes of conduct, and ethics should be bifurcated from the functions of training, education, accreditation, and capacity building.[1] Learning from the practices in other countries, separate boards could be established to deal with these different responsibilities and to avoid conflicts of interest and to improve efficiency. A regular review of the regulatory framework and performance in terms of upholding standards, disciplinary action, and accreditation process could also be considered by the concerned ministry or a separate co-regulatory body in this sector. As discussed in the literature on regulation and drawing upon the trends worldwide, a gradual move toward co-regulation with more active involvement by the state and mechanisms for competitive regulation through the allocation of some functions to separate boards may be warranted in the Indian context.

In addition, the representation process in the regulatory body needs to be more expertise-led by including some ex officio members who are independent experts, academics, and retired practitioners, and an attempt should be made to cover all sections of the sector-litigation, advisory, corporate, and noncorporate. This would allow the decision-making process to have a more long-term perspective on issues. A well-informed representative and expertise-driven regulator would also give more confidence to stakeholders about regulatory capacity. The experiences of other countries, their regulatory models, and criteria for membership in the regulatory body could be looked at when reviewing the regulator's framework.

Strengthening Governance

Given the widespread perception that the current regulatory framework suffers from weak governance of law firms and that little is done to discipline and debar those who are in violation of the rules and disciplines governing this sector, on a priority basis, steps have to be taken to ensure that contravention of existing regulations

---

[1] To what extent this would mean assigning part of the responsibility of training and education to the Ministry of Human Resource and Development is a difficult question to address given the turf issues between professional associations and the education ministry that have occurred in other professions such as medicine.

can be addressed through the existing disciplinary mechanism. If this is not possible, then legislation must be amended in order to strengthen the ambit of the disciplinary mechanism accordingly. This is pertinent to both domestic and foreign firms.

As this concern is very strong in the context of FLFs, if foreign commercial presence continues to be restricted, then the regulatory oversight mechanism over their tie-ups in India needs to be strengthened. This can be done by putting conditions on domestic firms in terms of who they can partner with and placing regular reporting requirements on their transactions, finances, clients, and their transactional relationship with the foreign firms so as to enable greater transparency and monitoring of their affiliations and providing the basis for initiating disciplinary action, if so needed. If foreign commercial presence is allowed, then eligibility conditions and post-entry conditions can be imposed and practice should be allowed only subject to the firm being formally recognized by the regulator, so that all regulations and disciplinary mechanisms applicable to domestic firms can also be applied to foreign firms. By introducing "behind-the-border" regulatory requirements as other countries have done on foreign firms, governance can be improved and reciprocity can be maintained.

Further, if governance and disciplinary mechanisms have to be strengthened, clarity will be required on what is allowed, what is proscribed, and the associated penalties. As noted earlier, the governance problem in the case of surrogate or affiliate firms arises in large part from the lack of clarity about what constitutes foreign legal practice and what is permitted under affiliate arrangements. These ambiguities are partly responsible for the fear that existing restrictions will be undermined if foreign firms are allowed to practice.

Preparing the Sector

If the sector has to be prepared to become more global and to face emerging challenges as well as reap the benefits from emerging opportunities, then constraints which currently hurt its growth prospects have to be alleviated. In addition, proactive measures have to be taken to promote capacity building and competitiveness.

However, these measures should be taken in conjunction with the aforementioned regulatory safeguards and steps to improve governance.

Relaxing Regulatory Restrictions

It has been noted earlier that restrictions on size, though often cited as a barrier to the growth of Indian law firms, have not been a major impediment and are no longer a constraint now with the enactment of the Companies Act, 2013 and the LLP Act, 2008. However, if we look at the future perspective, then restrictions on whom the lawyers can make partnerships with, is a constraint to those firms which aspire to become truly global and have the potential to do so.

Looking ahead at the emerging trends and requirements of businesses, there is a need to encourage the formation of multidisciplinary firms. If Indian firms are to be able to compete globally, then they must eventually be able to provide a wide range of integrated services. At present, under the LLP, the scope for setting up multidisciplinary firms remains restricted to CAs, cost accountants, and companies secretaries. To enable truly multidisciplinary firms, changes in other legislations, such as the Advocates Act will be needed to enable partnership between legal professionals for example and other professionals.

The existing restrictions on advertisement must be removed. Although this is a profession that relies more on trust and reputation and not per se active marketing and soliciting, the existing restrictions on advertising do, to some extent, put Indian law firms at a disadvantage vis-à-vis foreign firms, which are allowed to advertise quite freely. India could introduce similar legislation which allows firms to advertise their expertise and services, subject to their avoiding negative publicity of other firms or exaggerated claims about their own services. Again, keeping in mind future requirements and the need to strengthen the domestic firms, allowing them to advertise could potentially facilitate tie-ups, access to foreign markets, and access to new clients. It could also facilitate the outsourcing of legal services from other countries and benefit the LPO industry. As steps have already been taken to relax the advertising restrictions, India's advertising regulations could be brought in line with that followed in most other countries without much delay.

There is also need for a coordinated and comprehensive perspective of legislation and proposed amendments. The earlier discussion of various legislations and amendments in this sector indicates that the approach is often piecemeal, resulting in lack of clarity about the implications of legislations. An integrated perspective and approach to legislative reforms is needed if Indian firms are to be made globally competitive. This will also require inter-institutional coordination between the Ministry of Law and Justice, the Ministry of Corporate Affairs, and the Bar Council in consultation with state-level councils and different sections of the legal fraternity.

Capacity Building Measures

Proactive steps can also be taken to develop competence in the sector and to address the long-term interests of firms. On the education and training front, more emphasis could be put on CPD, periodic evaluations, and requirement to renew licenses based on some qualifying exam after every few years to ensure upgrading of standards by individual professionals, regular upgrading of curricula by training institutions, introduction of flexible formats of training for practitioners to enable part-time, online and weekend courses, developing specialized skill sets and domain expertise and on practical training. Training of trainers needs to be undertaken to improve the quality of teaching faculty in law schools beyond the premier institutions. For such major capacity-building initiatives, consultations are needed with independent experts, academics, practitioners, and government in order to devise a suitable training curriculum and to develop continuing licensing requirements. Alongside such steps, if lack of reciprocity is indeed a big impediment to market access, then the state and the regulator must proactively negotiate MRAs with other countries at least in selected segments of the profession and also push for effective reciprocity under MRAs.

Some possibilities could also be considered to make opening up of the sector beneficial from the training and education perspective. For instance, if the sector is opened up to foreign firms in future the government could make some amount of investment in training and capacity development of Indian professionals, a pre-condition for the entry of foreign firms. Or, the latter could be asked to apportion a certain part of their revenue/profit toward the development of legal training and professional development, before repatriating their profits to the parent organizations. There is a scope to link training and professional development requirements with the presence of FLFs.

There were also some recommendations regarding initiatives that need to be taken by Indian law firms. These pertained to becoming more global and professional in their outlook and investing more in technology, training, human resource management, information systems, and emerging areas of specialization so as to improve their standards and to take advantage of emerging opportunities in the domestic and global markets. Respondents also emphasized the need to clarify what is meant by opening up the sector as all other issues of regulation, reciprocity, level playing field, naturally flow from having a clear definition of what opening up would entail and hence to what extent various concerns and apprehensions are justified.

A Timeline for Reforms

In sum, the legal services sector in India requires reforms at various levels. The immediate focus over the next 3 to 5 years should be on strengthening the capacity by removing those restrictions which are not serving any purpose or have already become ineffective due to other changes in the sector and upgrading education and training requirements. Simultaneously, over the medium term, the regulatory structure needs to be strengthened along the lines highlighted earlier. These changes should go hand in hand with changes in legislation, removal of restrictions, and skilling and training initiatives undertaken to enhance capacity. Consistency and coordination in approach are required.

Once domestic firms are better equipped to deal with foreign competition and the governance framework has been strengthened, the sector could be opened up to foreign firms, but supported by well thought out regulatory requirements and conditions on their establishment and operations post entry. A broad strategy of phased liberalization could be considered to give time to Indian firms to develop internal capacity over a transition period of 5–10 years.

However, opening up need not be on a full scale and should be undertaken on a stage-by-stage basis, where an impact assessment is done after each phase and the strategy calibrated as required. Moreover, limitations and conditions can be placed alongside liberalization, as other countries have done. For instance, the scope of practice for FLFs could be restricted to home and third country/international law, while practice of domestic law would be reserved for domestic firms. It could be restricted to the corporate advisory segment, with litigation reserved for domestic law firms and domestic lawyers. Services and transactions where small firms dominate could be carved out to protect the latter's interests and some sectors/types of activities where it may be desirable for domestic firms to develop expertise or scale their operations could be excluded, at least for an interim transition period. At the same time, domestic lawyers working in international firms could be restricted from doing litigation and practicing domestic law so as to keep the boundaries between domestic and foreign firms clear even if nationals are employed. Additional conditions could be imposed on foreign firms, such as through quantitative restrictions on the hiring of local lawyers, limits on the number of licenses granted for setting up offices, placing a time restriction between setting up additional offices, introducing strict eligibility criteria for obtaining license to set up an office in India (subject to justification on economic or social grounds, nature of work, past experience, etc.) and introducing requirements for knowledge transfer, investment in training and education on foreign firms. The government and the regulator could look at other economies such as China, Singapore, and Malaysia to learn from their experiences with opening up legal services and regulating foreign firms and how these countries safeguarded their domestic interests in the wake of liberalization.

Several possible formats can be considered for liberalization, again drawing upon the experience of other countries and available models of operation. For instance, JVs between domestic and foreign firms could be encouraged to allay concerns over employment and business displacement. Foreign equity participation could be limited initially and gradually increased over a 10 year transition period.[2] The eligibility criteria for JVs could be based on reputation, past work, number of years of experience, tax returns and the like and the number of licenses to be issued to firms meeting these criteria could be restricted and frozen for 5–10 years till an impact assessment can be done. Formal and transparent partnerships with Indian firms where profit sharing is permitted and which can be regulated under existing rules could also be considered.

While the immediate need in India's legal sector is capacity building and strengthening, a possible roadmap for eventual opening up of the sector must also be kept in mind. As is evident, opening up does not mean deregulation of the sector. Opening up would re-regulation and ensuring well-regulated foreign competition in the domestic market while also protecting the interests of domestic firms. The liberalization process should therefore be gradual and phased and supported by regulatory reforms so that domestic firms are able to compete on an even footing with foreign firms and also have sufficient capacity to derive possible benefits that can result from opening up. The experience of other countries such as Singapore and Malaysia should be used to guide our strategy. It may be necessary to constitute a joint committee of the government and the professional association or an independent commission to work out a roadmap for reforms and liberalization and give recommendations to the government. Otherwise, there is a risk that the current inertia that is holding back much needed reforms will continue as no incumbent institution may be willing to "bite the bullet" and initiate change in this sector.

---

[2] It is important to note that JVs have not been successful in all countries. Experience suggests that they work if there is a very close relationship between partners but not if the arrangements are loose (as was the case in Singapore).

Annexure

Table A.1
OECD Services Trade Restrictiveness Index (STRI) Regulations for Legal Services

Policy Area	Regulations
Restrictions on foreign entry	Maximum foreign equity share (%)
	Equity restrictions apply to non-locally licensed professionals/firms
	Legal form: sole proprietorship is prohibited
	Corporation is prohibited
	Partnership is prohibited
	Commercial association is prohibited between fully integrated practitioners and other professionals
	Commercial association is prohibited between not fully integrated practitioners and fully integrated professionals
	Prohibitions on hiring locally-licensed lawyers
	Number of firms restricted by quotas
	Board of directors: majority must be nationals
	Board of directors: majority must be residents
	Board of directors: at least one must be national
	Board of directors: at least one must be resident
	Manager must be national
	Manager must be resident
	Board of directors: majority must be locally-licensed professionals
	Board of directors: at least one must be a locally-licensed professional
	Manager must be locally-licensed professional

(Table A.1 Continued)

(Table A.1 Continued)

Policy Area	Regulations
	Establishment of foreign firms restricted by economic needs tests
	Memo - Majority of shareholders must be locally-licensed
	Other restrictions on foreign entry
Restrictions on movement of people	Quotas: intra-corporate transferees
	Quotas: contractual services suppliers
	Quotas: independent services suppliers
	Labour market tests: intra-corporate transferees
	Labour market tests: contractual services suppliers
	Labour market tests: independent services suppliers
	Limitation on stay for intra-corporate transferees (months)
	Limitation on stay for contractual services suppliers (months)
	Limitation on stay for independent services suppliers (months)
	Nationality or citizenship required for license to practice
	Prior or permanent residency required for license to practice
	Prior or permanent residency required for license to practice under a limited license
	Domicile required for license to practice as a fully integrated lawyer
	Domicile required for license to practice under a limited license
	Laws or regulations establish a process for recognising higher education degrees in law earned abroad
	Foreign lawyers are required to take local examinations to qualify for full membership in law the profession
	Foreign lawyers are required to practice locally for at least 1 year in order to become a member of the profession
	Compulsory membership in a professional association for foreign lawyers is automatically granted if the lawyer has the required qualifications
	A limited licensing system is available
	Foreign providers have to completely re-do the university degree, practice and exam in the domestic country
	Other restrictions to movement of people

(Table A.1 Continued)

(Table A.1 Continued)

Policy Area	Regulations
Other discriminatory measures	Foreign suppliers treated less favorably regarding taxes and eligibility for subsidies
	There are limitations on foreign participation in public procurement
	Formal requirement to consider international standards/rules before setting new domestic standards
	Use of foreign firm names is prohibited
	Use of foreign firm names is allowed only alongside that of a local partner
	Only locally-licensed lawyers may use the name/title "Lawyer"
	Other restrictions in other discriminatory measures
Barriers to competition	Available appeal procedures in domestic regulatory systems are also open to affected foreign parties
	Foreign firms have redress when business practices are perceived to restrict competition
	Mandatory minimum and/or maximum fees
	Recommended minimum and/or maximum fees
	Advertising is either prohibited or subject to restrictions
	Only locally licensed professionals may advertise and market their services
	Other restrictions in barriers to competition
Regulatory transparency	Regulations are communicated to the public prior to entry into force
	Public comment procedure open to interested persons, including foreign suppliers
	Range of visa processing time (business days)
	Time to complete all official procedures to register a company (days)
	Cost to complete all official procedures for registering a company (% of income per capita)
	Number of official procedures for registering a company
	Other restrictions in regulatory transparency

Source: OECD Services Trade Restrictiveness Index Regulatory Database.

Table A.2
World Bank Modal Restrictions in Legal Services for Selected Countries

Country	Label	Mode 1	Mode 3	Mode 4
Australia	Legal Advice Foreign Law	Allowed, but legal documents must be signed by licensed lawyers.	There are no limits on ownership or control by foreign nationals, but the acquisition of substantial interests by foreigners must be notified. Notification thresholds are AUD 5 million and AUD 10 million for establishment of a new business. At least one equity partner of a foreign firm established in the states of VIC and NSW must be a permanent resident. In QLD, at least one equity partner must be resident for at least 180 days per calendar year. Ownership of law firms by non-lawyers, including corporations and stock market shareholders, is permitted.	Automatic recognition of foreign licenses is granted, subject to obtaining a "limited license", which can be obtained after proper registration of home license. Commercial association with local firms and lawyers is permitted except in SA (out of a total of six states and two territories), where natural persons practicing foreign law may only join a local law firm as a consultant and may not enter into partnership with or employ local lawyers. Temporary practice (90 days within a one-year period) is allowed without local registration of the home license. Foreign-licensed professionals are subject to LMT. Lawyers are on the skills shortage list. There is a minimum wage/wage parity requirement.
	Legal Advice Domestic Law		There are no limits on ownership or control by foreign nationals, but the acquisition of substantial interests by foreigners must be notified. Notification thresholds are AUD 5 million in an existing business and AUD 10 million for	Foreign-licensed professionals are eligible to practice, subject to certain conditions. Applicants must have a practice certificate (full license). 1) There is an education requirement; foreign degrees may be accepted, subject to evaluation. 2) There is a training requirement;

		establishment of a new business. Ownership of law firms by nonlawyers, including corporations and stock market shareholders, is permitted.	applicants must complete a practical training course. Foreign work experience may be taken into account by the Law Admissions Consultative Committee of Australia. 3) Passing a local examination is required. LMT. There is a minimum wage/wage parity requirement.
	Legal Representation in Court	There are no limits on ownership or control by foreign nationals, but the acquisition of substantial interests by foreigners must be notified. Notification thresholds are AUD 5 million in an existing business and AUD 10 million for establishment of a new business. Ownership of law firms by non-lawyers, including corporations and stock market shareholders, is permitted. Natural persons practicing foreign law may not enter into partnership with or employ local lawyers.	Foreign-licensed professionals are eligible to practice, subject to certain conditions. Applicants must have a practice certificate (full license). 1) There is an education requirement; foreign degrees may be accepted, subject to evaluation by the Law Admissions Consultative Committee of Australia (LACC). 2) There is a training requirement; applicants must obtain a certificate of completion from a preadmission practical training course, or complete a period of traineeship or tutorship with a practicing solicitor or barrister. The required length of the period varies by jurisdiction. Foreign work experience may be taken into account by the LACC. 3) Passing a local examination is required. LMT; hiring firm may have to prove its efforts to recruit and train nationals, and/or

(Table A.2 Continued)

(Table A.2 Continued)

Country	Label	Mode 1	Mode 3	Mode 4
Australia				its inability to recruit required personnel locally. However labor market and skills testing may be waived for certain key activities. There is a minimum wage/wage parity requirement. Employer sponsorship by a business operating lawfully in Australia, or a bona fide overseas business with a contract for the supply of a service, is required.
China	Legal Advice Foreign Law	Allowed.	Only representative offices (branches) are allowed; a separate legal entity is not allowed. There is a difference in licensing criteria for foreign and domestic applicants, in that a foreign firm must be licensed and have been operating legally in its home jurisdiction, have practiced there for at least two years, and be in need of establishing a Chinese office to carry out legal services. The chief representative must have practiced outside of China for at least three years, and be a partner of the parent firm. A representative office cannot hire locally-licensed attorneys.	Two years' work experience is required (three for chief representatives), which must have been acquired outside of China. Entry is possible only as an ICT. There is a minimum wage requirement; an employer shall not pay foreigners less than the local minimum wage. An ICT must reside in China for at least six months per year.

	Legal Advice Domestic Law		Not allowed.
	Legal Representation in Court		Not allowed.
India	Legal Advice Foreign Law	Not allowed.	Automatic recognition of foreign licenses is granted. Entry as an ICT or an SSE is possible. There is no limit on the duration of stay initially allowed; extensions are possible.
	Legal Advice Domestic Law		Applicants must become members of the Bar Council of India. They must have a law degree from a university in India (3 years of study for LLB degree) and pass an examination. Entry as an ICT or an SSE is possible. There is no limit on the duration of stay initially allowed; extensions are possible.
	Legal Representation in Court		Not allowed.
Japan	Legal Advice Foreign Law	Not allowed. Services must be supplied through qualified natural person or commercial presence.	Both branches and separate legal entities are not allowed. A joint venture between a foreign legal consultant and local lawyers is permitted. A law firm must take the form of a sole proprietorship or quasi-partnership. A foreign firm is limited to establishing one local office.	Foreign licensed professionals must meet certain conditions. Registration as a "gaikokuho-jimu-bengoshi" (registered foreign lawyer) with the Japan Federation of Bar Association is necessary, which requires the approval of the Minister of Justice. Subject to reciprocity, but the requirement isn't applied

(Table A.2 Continued)

(Table A.2 Continued)

Country	Label	Mode 1	Mode 3	Mode 4
Japan			Ownership or control by non-locally-licensed professionals is not permitted since one must be registered as a "gaikokuho-jimu-bengoshi" or a "bengoshi" in Japan and may not be a juridical person. Hiring locally licensed professionals as employees is not permitted. A foreign legal consultant may use the name of the foreign firm with which he/she is affiliated, but reference must be made to "gaikokuho-jimu-bengoshi-jimusho."	to WTO members. 1) Residency: applicants are required to establish residence once qualification is granted. 2) At least three years of work experience from the home country are required. Service suppliers must stay in Japan for at least 180 days in a year.
	Legal Advice Domestic Law		Both branches and separate legal entities are not allowed. Services must be supplied by a natural person or a Legal Profession Corporation. A joint venture between a foreign legal consultant and local lawyers is permitted on a permanent basis, but local lawyers in this case must have more than five years of practical experience. A foreign firm is limited to establishing one local office. Ownership	Foreign licensed professionals must meet certain conditions. They need to be registered as a "bengoshi" with the Japan Federation of Bar Associations. 1) Residency: applicants are required to establish residence once qualification is granted. 2) Two years of training at the Legal Training and Research Institute are required; this must be done in Japan. 3) Pass a local examination. Service suppliers must stay in Japan for at least 180 days in a year.

		or control by non-locally-licensed professionals is not permitted since one must be registered as a "gaikokuho-jimu-bengoshi" or a "bengoshi" in Japan and may not be a juridical person. Hiring locally-licensed professionals as employees is not permitted. A foreign legal consultant may use the name of the foreign firm with which he/she is affiliated, but reference must be made to "gaikokuho-jimu-bengoshi-jimusho."	Foreign licensed professionals must meet certain conditions. They need to be registered as a "bengoshi" with the Japan Federation of Bar Associations. 1) Residency: applicants are required to establish residence once qualification is granted. 2) Two years of training at the Legal Training and Research Institute are required; this must be done in Japan. 3) Pass a local examination. Service suppliers must stay in Japan for at least 180 days in a year.
	Legal Representation in Court	A branch is not allowed. Services must be supplied by a natural person or a Legal Profession Corporation. A joint venture between a foreign legal consultant and local lawyers is permitted on a permanent basis, but local lawyers in this case must have more than five years of practical experience. A foreign firm is limited to establishing one local office. Ownership or control by non-locally-licensed professionals is not permitted, since one must be registered as a "gaikokuho-jimu-bengoshi" or a "bengoshi" in Japan and	

(Table A.2 Continued)

(Table A.2 Continued)

Country	Label	Mode 1	Mode 3	Mode 4
Japan			may not be a juridical person. Hiring locally-licensed professionals as employees is not permitted. A foreign legal consultant may use the name of the foreign firm with which he/she is affiliated, but reference must be made to "gaikokuho-jimu-bengoshi-jimusho."	
Malaysia	Legal Advice Foreign Law	Allowed, as long as the foreign firm is staffed with professionals licensed to provide the service desired.	Not allowed. Exceptions include corporations incorporated in the Federal Territory of Labuan which can only provide services to offshore corporations established in the Federal Territory of Labuan.	Not allowed, but ad hoc, special admission may be given to foreign-licensed lawyers with at least seven years of experience to appear before a court in Malaysia. The lawyer must have qualifications or experience not available in Malaysia.
	Legal Advice Domestic Law		Not allowed. Exceptions include corporations incorporated in the Federal Territory of Labuan which can only provide services to offshore corporations established in the Federal Territory of Labuan.	Not allowed, but ad hoc, special admission may be given to foreign-licensed lawyers with at least seven years of experience to appear before a court in Malaysia. The lawyer must have qualifications or experience not available in Malaysia.

	Legal Representation in Court		Not allowed. Exceptions include corporations incorporated in the Federal Territory of Labuan which can only provide services to offshore corporations established in the Federal Territory of Labuan.	Not allowed, but ad hoc, special admission may be given to foreign-licensed lawyers with at least seven years of experience to appear before a court in Malaysia. The lawyer must have qualifications or experience not available in Malaysia.
The United Kingdom	Legal Advice Foreign Law	Allowed, except that service providers must comply with local codes of ethics, use their home title, attend to insurance requirements, complete a simplified admission to the Bar through an aptitude test, and have a legal domicile in the host country.	Allowed.	Automatic recognition of foreign licenses is granted. Foreign lawyers are permitted to practice as a foreign legal consultant under their home title, and it is assumed that they are regulated by their home state bar or law society. There is also a point-based visa program; points are awarded for education, prior earnings, age, UK experience, and English language proficiency. Foreign-licensed professionals are subject to LMT.
	Legal Advice Domestic Law		Commercial presence providing legal services on domestic (EC and Member states) law may take any of the legal forms allowed under the national law	Foreign-licensed professionals must meet certain conditions. 1) Residency in the UK may be necessary, due to the local training requirement. 2) There is an education

(Table A.2 Continued)

(Table A.2 Continued)

Country	Label	Mode 1	Mode 3	Mode 4
The United Kingdom			of the relevant Member State. For barristers, only sole proprietorship is acceptable. Lawyers practicing EC or Member state law must be fully qualified to provide the services.	requirement; foreign education is not recognized. 3) Two years of training in the UK may be required. 4) Passing a local examination is necessary (the QLTT aptitude test). There is also a point-based visa program; points are awarded for education, prior earnings, age, UK experience, and English language proficiency. Foreign-licensed professionals are subject to LMT.
	Legal Representation in Court		Allowed.	Foreign-licensed professionals must meet certain conditions. 1) Residency in the UK may be necessary, due to the local training requirement. 2) There is an education requirement; foreign education is not recognized. 3) Two years of training in the UK may be required. 4) Passing a local examination is necessary (the QLTT aptitude test). There is also a point-based visa program; points are awarded for education, prior earnings, age, UK experience, and English language proficiency. Foreign-licensed professionals are subject to LMT.

The United States of America	Legal Advice Foreign Law	Allowed, but legal documents must be signed by licensed lawyers (licensed in foreign law).	Non-locally-licensed professionals are not allowed to hold any ownership or control in a law firm.	Foreign-licensed professionals are eligible to practice subject to certain conditions: residency; work experience (up to five years in home jurisdiction may be required in some states); and a quota and labor market test (65,000 petition approvals in any fiscal year). There is a minimum wage/wage parity requirement.
	Legal Advice Domestic Law		Non-locally-licensed professionals are not allowed to hold any ownership or control in a law firm.	Applicants must become a member of the bar in the state whose law they intend to practice. The following requirements apply: 1) Residency. 2) Education: three years of postgraduate education in a US law school. Foreign degrees are not recognized. 3) Passing the bar examination is required. A quota and labor market test apply to foreign IP; the quota applies only to the H1-B visa category (specialty occupations), which includes professionals hired for a temporary period by a US firm (there are 65,000 petition approvals in any fiscal year). A Labor Condition Application by the US employer is required. There is a minimum wage/wage parity requirement. As a result of bilateral trade agreements, nationals from Australia, Singapore and Chile in special occupations, including accountants, auditors, and lawyers, can enter the US under additional, separate quotas.

(Table A.2 Continued)

(Table A.2 Continued)

Country	Label	Mode 1	Mode 3	Mode 4
The United States of America	Legal Representation in Court		Non-locally-licensed professionals are not allowed to hold any ownership or control in a law firm.	Applicants must become a member of the bar in the state whose law they intend to practice. The following requirements apply: 1) Residency: most states require current residency at the time of licensing as a lawyer, but not thereafter. 2) Education: three years of postgraduate education in a U.S. law school. Foreign degrees are not recognized. 3) Passing the bar examination is required. A quota and labor market test apply to foreign IP; the quota applies only to the H1-B visa category (specialty occupations), which includes professionals hired for a temporary period by a U.S. firm (there are 65,000 petition approvals in any fiscal year). A Labor Condition Application by the US employer is required. There is a minimum wage/wage parity requirement. As a result of bilateral trade agreements, nationals from Australia, Singapore and Chile in special occupations, including accountants, auditors, and lawyers, can enter the US under additional, separate quotas.

Source: http://iresearch.worldbank.org/servicetrade/home.htm (last accessed on January 1, 2015).

Table A.3
Entry and Conduct Regulations Used for Calculating OECD Indicator

	Topic Weight a_i	Sub-topic Weight b_j	Question Weight c_k	Coding of answers			
Entry regulation	½						
Exclusive or shared exclusive rights		1/4					
If access to the profession is regulated, how many services does the profession provide under an exclusive or shared exclusive right?			1	0/no license	1	2	3	>3
				0	1.5	3	4.5	6
Education requirements		1/4						
If access to the profession is regulated:								
What is the duration of special education/ university/ or other higher degree?			1/3	equals 0 if no license is required or the number of years of education (max of 6)				

(Table A.3 Continued)

(Table A.3 Continued)

	Topic Weight	Sub-topic Weight	Question Weight	
What is the duration of compulsory practice necessary to become a full member of the profession?			1/3	equals 0 if no license is required or the number of years of compulsory practice (max of 6)
Are there professional exams that must be passed to become a full member of the profession?			1/3	no/no license — yes 0 6
Compulsory chamber membership		1/4		
Membership in a professional organization is compulsory in order to legally practice			1	no — yes 0 6
Quotas		1/4		
Is the number of foreign professionals/firms permitted to practice restricted by quotas?			1	no — yes 0 6

Conduct regulation	1/2							
			no regulation	non-binding recommended prices for some services	non-binding recommended prices for all services	maximum prices for some services	maximum prices for all services	minimum prices for some services	minimum prices for all services
The fees or prices that a profession charges are regulated by the government or self-regulated		1/4	0	1	2	3	4	5	6
Regulation on advertising and marketing by professional services		1/4	no restrictions 0			restricted 3			Prohibited 6
Regulation of the legal form of business		1/4	no restrictions 0	some incorporation allowed	most forms allowed 2		incorporation forbidden 5		sole practitioner only 6
Regulation of inter-professional cooperation		1/4	all forms allowed 0		most forms allowed 3		allowed between comparable professions 4.5		generally forbidden 6
Country scores (0–6)						$\Sigma a_i \Sigma b_j \Sigma c_k \text{answer}_{ijk}$			

Source: OECD Indicators of Product Market Regulation.

Table A.4
Legal Services Commitments by Korea in India–Korea CEPA

Sector or Sub-sector	Limitations on Market Access	Limitations on National Treatment	Additional Commitments
a. Legal services; (CPC 861*)[a] Advisory Services on law of the jurisdiction where service supplier is qualified as a lawyer and on public international law, excluding the following: (i) representation for juridical or statutory procedures in courts and other government agencies as well as preparation of legal documents for such procedures; (ii) legal representation for the entrustment of the preparation of notarial deeds; (iii) those activities concerning a legal case whose objective is the acquisition or loss or change of rights concerning real property in Korea, intellectual property rights, mining rights or other rights arising upon registration thereof with government agencies in Korea; and	1) None 2) None 3) Only in the form of representative office. Association with or employment of local lawyers with Korean qualification or equivalent is not permitted. 4) Unbound except as indicated in the Horizontal Commitments section. Commercial presence is required.	1) None 2) None 3) Foreign legal consultants are required to stay in Korea not less than 180 days per year. 4) Unbound except as indicated in the Horizontal Commitments section.	1) Representation in international commercial arbitration is permitted, provided that the applicable procedural and substantive laws in the arbitration are the laws which the foreign legal consultant is qualified to practice in Korea. 2) Use of firm name is permitted, provided that it is used with reference to "Foreign legal consultants office" in Korean

	(iv) legal cases concerning family relations or inheritance, in which a Korean national is involved as a party or the property concerned is located in Korea.

Source: India–Korea CEPA document.
Notes: The following information is provided for transparency purposes only:

1. A foreign lawyer who wishes to practice law as a foreign legal consultant in Korea must register with the Korean Bar Association, must have practiced law for at least 3 years in the jurisdiction where he/she is qualified as a lawyer, and must be in good standing of the legal profession in the jurisdiction.
2. Permission of the Minister of Justice is required for the establishment of a representative office in Korea. The representative office consists of a FLC or FLCs approved by the Minister of Justice. It must have credibility and expertise, and sufficient capability to compensate for damages caused to the client, if any. The chief of the representative office must have practiced law for at least 7 years, including 3 years in the jurisdiction of his/her qualification.
3. A representative office can conduct profit-making activities provided that such presence in Korea maintains proper business plans and financial bases.
4. For the purpose of the commitment to this sector, only the law firm which is organized under India's relevant law and headquartered in India can establish its representative office in Korea.

[a] An asterisk on the CPC Code number indicates that the corresponding service sub-sector in this schedule only covers a part or parts of the service sub-sector classified under the given CPC code number and the specific commitments for that code shall not extend to the total range of services covered under that code.

Table A.5
Legal Services Commitments by Japan in India–Japan CEPA

Sector or Subsector	Limitations on Market Access	Limitations on National Treatment	Additional Commitments
Legal services supplied by a lawyer qualified as "Bengoshi" under Japanese law (861)	1) None except that: services must be supplied by a natural person or by a Legal Profession corporation1[a]; and commercial presence is required. 2) None except that: services must be supplied by a natural person or by a Legal Profession Corporation; and commercial presence is required. 3) None except that services must be supplied by a natural person or by a Legal Profession Corporation. 4) None except that commercial presence is required.	1) None 2) None 3) None 4) None	
Legal advisory services on law of jurisdiction where the service supplier is a qualified lawyer (861**)[b] (a) Legal advisory services on law do not include:	1) None except that: services must be supplied by a natural person; and commercial presence is required. 2) None	1) None except that a service supplier is required to stay in Japan not less than 180 days in a year.	1) Practice of international law is permitted, provided that the international law is or was in force in the jurisdiction. Practice

(i) legal representational services for juridical procedures in courts and other government agencies as well as preparation of legal documents for such procedures; (ii) expression of legal opinions concerning laws other than laws of the jurisdiction where the service supplier is qualified as a lawyer (hereinafter referred to in this sector as "the jurisdiction"); (iii) legal representational services for the entrustment of the preparation of notarial deeds; and (iv) those activities concerning a legal case whose primary objective is the acquisition or loss or change of rights concerning real property in Japan or of industrial property rights, mining rights or other rights arising upon registration thereof with government agencies in Japan.	3) None except that services must be supplied by a natural person. 4) None except that commercial presence is required.	2) None 3) None 4) None except that a service supplier is required to stay in Japan not less than 180 days in a year.	of third country law is permitted, according to written advice on each issue from competent persons (e.g. lawyers qualified in the third country and engaging in legal business concerning the law of that country). Practice of Japanese law is not permitted. 2) Association with Bengoshi is permitted. Employment of Bengoshi is permitted. 3) Use of firm name is unrestricted, provided that it is followed with reference to "Gaikoku-Ho-Jimu-Bengoshi Jimusho". 4) Representation in international arbitration is permitted.

(Table A.5 Continued)

(Table A.5 Continued)

Sector or Subsector	Limitations on Market Access	Limitations on National Treatment	Additional Commitments
(b)	A service supplier shall be required to cooperate with Bengoshi or to ask for his/her advice in a legal case concerning family relations or inheritance, in which a Japanese national is involved as a party, or in a legal case whose objective is the acquisition or loss or change of rights concerning real property in Japan or of industrial property rights, mining rights or other rights arising upon registration thereof with government agencies in Japan, as long as the above objective is not the primary one.		

Note to the Specific Commitment in the Sector of Legal Advisory Services on Law of Jurisdiction where the Service Supplier is a Qualified Lawyer

The service supplier must be recognized as "Gaikoku-Ho-Jimu-Bengoshi" by the Minister of Justice and register with the Japan Federation of Bar Associations.

The conditions for granting recognition by the Minister of Justice are as follows:

1. The service supplier is qualified as a lawyer in the jurisdiction.
2. The service supplier has been engaged as a lawyer for at least three years in the jurisdiction.
3. The service supplier is not subject to such conditions of disqualification in the jurisdiction which, if applied to "Bengoshi", would disqualify the "Bengoshi".

4. The service supplier possesses the intention to undertake the profession in good faith.
5. The service supplier possesses plans, residence and financial basis to perform his/her functions properly and steadily.
6. The service supplier possesses capability to compensate for damages caused to the client, if any.

Legal services supplied by a judicial scrivener qualified as "Shiho-Shoshi" under Japanese Law (861**)	1) None except that: services must be supplied by a natural person or by a Judicial Scrivener Corporation; and commercial presence is required. 2) None except that: Services must be supplied by a natural person or by a Judicial Scrivener Corporation; and commercial presence is required. 3) None except that services must be supplied by a natural person or by a Judicial Scrivener Corporation. 4) None except that commercial presence is required.	1) None 2) None 3) None 4) None
Legal services supplied by an administrative scrivener qualified as "Gyousei-Shoshi" under Japanese law (861**)	1) None except that: services must be supplied by a natural person or by an Administrative Scrivener Corporation; And commercial presence is required. 2) None except that: services must be supplied by a natural person or by an Administrative Scrivener	1) None 2) None 3) None 4) None

(Table A.5 Continued)

(Table A.5 Continued)

Sector or Subsector	Limitations on Market Access	Limitations on National Treatment	Additional Commitments
Legal services supplied by an administrative scrivener qualified as "Gyousei-Shoshi" under Japanese law (861**)	3) Corporation; and commercial presence is required. 4) None except that services must be supplied by a natural person or by an Administrative Scrivener Corporation. 4) None except that commercial presence is required.		
Legal services supplied by a certified social insurance and labour consultant qualified as "Shakai-Hoken-Romushi" under Japanese law (861**)	1) None except that: services must be supplied by a natural person or by a Certified Social Insurance and Labour Consultant Corporation; and commercial presence is required. 2) None except that: services must be supplied by a natural person or by a Certified Social Insurance and Labour Consultant Corporation; and commercial presence is required. 3) None except that services must be supplied by a natural person or by	1) None 2) None 3) None 4) None	

	a Certified Social Insurance and Labour Consultant Corporation. 4) None except that commercial presence is required.	
Legal services supplied by a patent attorney qualified as "Benrishi" under Japanese law (86119, 8612, 8613, 8619)	1) None except that: services must be supplied by a natural person or by a Patent Business Corporation; and commercial presence is required for a Patent Business Corporation. 2) None except that: services must be supplied by a natural person or by a Patent Business Corporation; and commercial presence is required for a Patent Business Corporation. 3) None except that services must be supplied by a natural person or by a Patent Business Corporation. 4) None	1) None 2) None 3) None 4) None
Legal services supplied by a maritime procedure agent qualified as "Kaijidairishi" under Japanese law (861**)	1) None except that services must be supplied by a natural person. 2) None except that services must be supplied by a natural person. 3) None except that services must be supplied by a natural person. 4) None	1) None 2) None 3) None 4) None

(Table A.5 Continued)

(Table A.5 Continued)

Sector or Subsector	Limitations on Market Access	Limitations on National Treatment	Additional Commitments
Legal services supplied by a land and house surveyor qualified as "Tochi-Kaoku-Chosashi" under Japanese law (861**)	1) None except that: services must be supplied by a natural person or by a Land and House Surveyor Corporation; And commercial presence is required. 2) None except that: services must be supplied by a natural person or by a Land and House Surveyor Corporation; and commercial presence is required. 3) None except that services must be supplied by a natural person or by a Land and House Surveyor Corporation. 4) None except that commercial presence is required.	1) None 2) None 3) None 4) None	

Source: India–Japan CEPA document.

Notes: [a] A Legal Profession Corporation under Japanese law is composed of one or more partners who are lawyers qualified as "Bengoshi" under Japanese law and have the rights and obligations to execute activities of the Legal Profession Corporation.
[b] Double asterisks on the CPC Code number indicates that the corresponding service sub-sector in this schedule only covers a part or parts of the service sub-sector classified under the given CPC code number and the specific commitments for that code shall not extend to the total range of services covered under that code.

Table A.6
Legal Services Commitments by Singapore in India–Singapore CECA

Sector or Subsector	Limitations on Market Access	Limitations on National Treatment	Additional Commitments
Legal consultancy services for Indian law (861**)[a]	1) Unbound 2) None 3) Unbound 4) Unbound except as indicated in the horizontal section	1) Unbound 2) None 3) Unbound 4) Unbound	

Source: India–Singapore CECA.

Notes: [a] Double asterisks on the CPC Code number indicates that the corresponding service sub-sector in this schedule only covers a part or parts of the service sub-sector classified under the given CPC code number and the specific commitments for that code shall not extend to the total range of services covered under that code.

Bibliography

Primary Resources

Abugattas Majluf, L., and S. Zarrilli. "Challenging Conventional Wisdom: Development Implications of Trade in Services Liberalization." UNCTAD and United Nations. New York and Geneva, 2007.

Acritas Sharplegal. "Global Elite Brand Index." http://www.acritas.com/GlobalEliteBrandIndex2014 (last accessed on January 1, 2015).

Arnould, R.J. and T.S. Friedland. "The Effect of Fee Schedules on the Legal Services Industry." *Journal of Human Resources* 11, no. 4 (1976): 258–265.

BCI Rules. 1975. http://www.barcouncilofindia.org/about/professional-standards/rules-on-professional-standards/ (last accessed on April 1, 2013).

BCI Websites. http://www.barcouncilofindia.org/about/about-the-legal-profession/legal-education-in-the-united-kingdom/; http://www.barcouncilofindia.org/about/about-the-bar-council-of-india/; http://www.barcouncilofindia.org/about/about-the-legal-profession/ (all accessed on April 1, 2013).

Chanda, R., and P. Gupta. "Services Reforms in India: Update and Challenges." In *Priorities and Pathways in Services Reform: Part II- Political Economy Studies*, edited by R. Findlay, 99-119. World Scientific, Singapore, 2013.

Chapman, M.J., and P.J. Tauber. "Liberalizing International Trade in Legal Services: A Proposal for an Annex on Legal Services Under The General Agreement on Trade In Services." *Michigan Journal of International Law* 16 (1995): 941–980.

Cheng, C.L.A. "Legal Systems in ASEAN – Singapore: Chapter 6 - The Legal Profession." (n.d.). http://www.aseanlawassociation.org/papers/sing_chp6.pdf (last accessed August 16, 2014).

Cohen, A.M. "International Law Firms in China: Market Access and Ethical Risks." *Fordham Law Review* 80, no. 6, Article 9 (2012).

Conway, P., and G. Nicoletti. "Product Market Regulation in non-manufacturing sectors in OECD countries: measurement and highlights" (working paper no. 530, OECD Economics Department, Paris, 2006).

Datamonitor. "Industry Profile: Global Legal Services." 2013. http://www.datamonitor.com/ (last accessed August 8, 2014).

Bibliography 193

Datamonitor. "Legal Services: Global Industry Guide." 2014. http://www.datamonitor.com/ (last accessed August 8, 2014).

Dingwall, R. and P. Fenn. "A Respectable Profession? A Sociological and Economic Perspective on the Regulation of Professions." *International Review of Law and Economics*, 7 (1987): 51–64

Economic Survey. Government of India. 2012–2013. http://indiabudget.nic.in/survey.asp (last accessed September 6, 2014).

Foreign Exchange Regulation Act. 1973. http://www.rbi.org.in/scripts/ECMUserView.aspx?Id=21&CatID=12 (last accessed September 6, 2014).

Goldberg, S.B. "South of the Border." *American Bar Association journal*, 80, March (1994): 74–77.

Hariani, A. "Foreign Law Firms in India." *Newsletter*, February 2, 2010.

Harvard Law School Program on the Legal Profession. "The Legal Profession of the People's Republic of China', Harvard Law School." 2011a. http://www.law.harvard.edu/programs/plp (last accessed August 1, 2014)

———. "The Japanese Legal Profession." 2011b. http://www.law.harvard.edu/programs/plp/pdf/Japanese_Legal_Profession.pdf (last accessed July 30, 2014).

———. "The Japanese Legal Profession." 2011c. http://www.law.harvard.edu/programs/plp/pdf/Japanese_Legal_Profession.pdf (last accessed July 30, 2014).

Hudec and Trebilcock . "Lawyer Advertising and the Supply of Information in the Market for Legal Services." *University of Western Ontario Law Review*, 20, no. 1 (1982): 53–99

Indo-UK Joint Economic & Trade Committee (JETCO) Report. February 2006. http://commerce.nic.in/pressrelease/pressrelease_detail.asp?id=710 (last accessed July 30, 2014).

Kuala Lumpur Bar Committee. "Pupillage Handbook Directory." http://www.klbar.org.my/files/Pupillage_Handbook_%26_Directory_%28Final%20Version%29.pdf (last accessed July 30, 2014).

Law Council of Australia. "Policy Statement on International Legal Practice." (n.d.). http://www.lawcouncil.asn.au/lawcouncil/images/LCA-PDF/a-z-docs/InternationalLegalPractice.pdf (last accessed July 30, 2014).

Love, J.H., and F.H. Stephen. "Advertising, Price and Quality in Self-regulating Professions: A Survey." *International Journal of the Economics of Business* 3, no. 2 (1996): 227–247.

"LPO as career for lawyers and law graduates, Outsource Portfolio." June 2, 2010. http://outsourceportfolio.com/lpo-career-lawyers-law-graduates/ (last accessed April 1, 2013).

OECD Sectoral Note. "STRI Sector Brief: Legal services." 2014. http://www.oecd.org/tad/services-trade/STRI_legal_services.pdf (last accessed August 18, 2014).

"OECD Services Trade Restrictiveness Index Regulatory Database." http://www.oecd.org/tad/services-trade/regulatory-database-services-trade-restrictiveness-index.htm (last accessed January 1, 2015).

"OECD Indicators of Product Market Regulation." http://www.oecd.org/eco/growth/indicatorsofproductmarketregulationhomepage.htm#indicators (last accessed January 1, 2015).

Ogus, A. "Rethinking Self-Regulation." *Oxford Journal of Legal Studies* 15 (1995): 97–108.

Paton, P.D. "Legal Services and the GATS: Norms as Barriers to Trade." *New England Journal of International and Comparative Law*, 9 no. 2, (2003): 361–416.

Sachdeva, S., and A.M. Sachdeva. "The Indian LLP Law: Some Concerns for Lawyers and CAS." *SEBI & Coporate Law*, 92, no. 6 (2009).

Schroeter, John Raymond, Scott L. Smith, and Steven R. Cox. "Advertising and Competition in Routine Legal Service Markets: An Empirical Investigation." *The Journal of Industrial Economics* 36, no. 1 (1987): 49–60.

Shaked, A., and J. Sutton. "The Self-Regulating Profession." *The Review of Economic Studies* 48, no. 2 (1981): 217–234.

Silver, C., Nicole De Bruin Phelan, and Mikaela Rabinowitz. "Between Diffusion and Distinctiveness in Globalization: US Law Firms Go Global." *Georgetown Journal of Legal Ethics* 22 (2009).

Silver, C. "What We Don't Know Can Hurt Us: The Need for Empirical Research in Regulating Lawyers and Legal Services in the Global Economy." *Akron Law Review* 43 (2010): 1009.

———. "Globalization and the US Market in Legal Services-Shifting Identities," (paper no. 409, Faculty Publications). http://www.repository.law.indiana.edu/facpub/409 (accessed on June 28, 2014).

Sim, T.Y.S. "A Guide to the Singapore Legal System and Legal Research." 2007. http://www.nyulawglobal.org/globalex/Singapore.htm (last accessed August 25, 2014).

Stephen, F.H., and C. Burns. "Liberalization of Legal Services." In *Service Liberalization in Europe: Case Studies*, edited by Aymo Brunetti and Sven Michal. Vol. 2. Berne: State Secretariate for Economic Affairs, 2007.

Stephen, F.H., and J.H. Love. "Regulation of the Legal Profession." In *Encyclopaedia of Law and Economics*, edited by Boudewijn Bouckaert and Gerrit De Geest. Cheltenham: Edward Elgar, 2000.

Terry, L.S. "The Future Regulation of the Legal Profession: The Impact of Treating the Legal Profession as 'Service Providers'." *Journal of Professional Lawyer* 2008 (2009): 189.

The Advocates Act. 1961. http://www.barcouncilofindia.org/wp-content/uploads/2010/05/Advocates-Act1961.pdf (last accessed September 24, 2014).

The Companies Act. 1956. http://www.mca.gov.in/Ministry/pdf/Companies_Act_1956_13jun2011.pdf (last accessed on July 20, 2014).

The Indian Partnership Act. 1932. http://www.mca.gov.in/Ministry/actsbills/pdf/Partnership_Act_1932.pdf (last accessed on August 1, 2014).

The Limited liability Partnership Act. 2008. http://www.mca.gov.in/Ministry/actsbills/pdf/LLP_Act_2008_15jan2009.pdf (last accessed on August 5, 2014).

The Malaysian Bar Press Release. "Foreign Law Firms and Foreign Lawyers Now Permitted to Practise in Peninsular Malaysia." June 30, 2014.

Tullao, T. "The Liberalization of Professional Services" (working paper series 1999–03, College of Business and Economics, CBE, De La Salle University, Philippines, 1999.

UN Services Trade Database. http://unstats.un.org/unsd/servicetrade/default.aspx (last accessed March 27, 2013).

ValueNotes Outsourcing Weekly. "Legal Outsourcing Hype: Can India Deliver." *ValueNotes Outsourcing Weekly,* October 6, 2006, III, no. 40.

Van den Bergh, R. "Towards Efficient Regulation in Markets for Professional Services." In *European Competition Law Annual 2004: The Relationship Between Competition Law and the (Liberal) Professions,* edited by Claus Dieter Ehlermann and Isabella Atanasiu, 155–176. Oxford and Portland: Hart Publishing.

Von Nordenflecht, A. "What is a Professional Service Firm? Toward a Theory and Taxonomy of Knowledge-Intensive Firms". *Academy of Management Review* 35, no. 1 (2010): 155–174

Wilkins, D. "Who Should Regulate Lawyers?" *Harvard Law Review,* 105, no. 4, (1992 February): 799–887.

World Bank Services Trade Restriction Database. http://iresearch.worldbank.org/servicestrade/ (last accessed March 27, 2013).

WTO. "Secretariat Background Note on Legal Services," *Note No: S/C/W/318,* WTO, USA, June 14, 2010.

———. "Secretariat Background Note on Legal Services," *Note No: S/C/W/43,* WTO, USA, July 6, 1998.

Yougov Survey. "Survey of India Market Opinion in association with Allen & Overy." 2012. http://www.allenovery.com/SiteCollectionDocuments/Time%20to%20liberalise%20India's%20legal%20market.pdf (last accessed April 15, 2013).

Web Resources

Country-wise Government, Regulatory Bodies, and other Web sites

1. Australia[1]
   - http://www.lawcouncil.asn.au/
   - http://www.alrc.gov.au/about
   - http://www.lawcouncil.asn.au/about/role.cfm
   - http://www.ag.gov.au/About/Pages/default.aspx
   - http://www.lawcouncil.asn.au/sections/legal-practice/
   - http://www.lawcouncil.asn.au/sections/international-law/
   - http://www.lawcouncil.asn.au/programs/national_profession/coag.cfm

---

[1] All the web sites accessed last on January 30, 2013.

- www.qls.com.au/files/...6263.../qls_factsheet_-_practice_structures.pdf
- http://www.ibanet.org/PPID/Constituent/Bar_Issues_Commission/ITILS_Australia.aspx
- http://www.lsb.vic.gov.au/legal-profession/working-under-the-act/professional-indemnity-insurance/
- http://www.law.unimelb.edu.au/masters/future-students/single-subject-study-cpd/continuing-professional-development-cpd

2. China[2]
   - http://www.hg.org/bar-associations-china.asp
   - http://english.cpc.people.com.cn/66102/6758183.html
   - http://www.chinalawsociety.com/index.asp?infoid=56
   - http://www.chinalawblog.com/basics-of-china-business-law/
   - http://www.chinadaily.com.cn/china/2011-12/25/content_14324123.htm
   - http://europe.chinadaily.com.cn/epaper/2012-10/05/content_15797119.htm
   - http://www.china.org.cn/business/laws_regulations/2007-06/22/content_1214778.htm
   - http://www.china-briefing.com/news/2012/02/07/foreign-law-firms-in-china-2012-listings.html
   - http://worldsavvy.org/monitor/index.php?option=com_content&view=article&id=113&Itemid=176
   - http://worldsavvy.org/monitor/index.php?option=com_content&view=article&id=113:legal-system&catid=54:keyplayersinternal&Itemid=176

4. India[3]
   - http://www.vakilbabu.com/System/JSystem2.htm
   - http://www.india.gov.in/spotlight/parliament-india-0
   - http://www.governmentofindia.org/executive-branch-in-india.htm
   - http://www.barcouncilofindia.org/bar-council-announces-proposed-directions-for-reform-in-legal-education/

5. Japan[4]
   - http://www.japan-guide.com/e/e2136.html
   - http://en.wikipedia.org/wiki/Barrister#Japan
   - http://www.moj.go.jp/ENGLISH/preface.html
   - http://www.nichibenren.or.jp/en/about/us/profile.html
   - http://www.gocurrency.com/articles/stories-japan-diet
   - http://www.courts.go.jp/english/system/system/index.html#01
   - http://www.japaneselawtranslation.go.jp/law/detail/?id=1878&vm=04&re=02

[2] All the web sites accessed last on January 29, 2013.
[3] All the web sites accessed last on April 1, 2013.
[4] All the web sites accessed last on January 29, 2013.

Bibliography 197

- http://www.lawcouncil.asn.au/lawcouncil/images/LCA-PDF/Country_Fact_Sheets/Japan.pdf
- http://onlinelaw.wustl.edu/major-differences-between-the-japanese-and-american-legal-systems/

6. Malaysia[5]
    - http://www.asdb.org.my/aboutus.html
    - http://www.muslim-lawyers.net/news/datoothman.html
    - http://www.state.gov/e/eb/rls/othr/ics/2012/191191.htm
    - http://www.malaysianbar.org.my/malaysian_court_system.html
    - http://www.lpqb.org.my/index.php?option=com_content&view=article&id=47&Itemid=61
    - http://www.bac.edu.my/index.php/why-study-law/20-career-options/attorney-generals-chambers
    - http://www.malaysianbar.org.my/trade_in_legal_services_formerly_known_as_gats/liberalisation_of_legal_services.html
    - http://www.freemalaysiatoday.com/category/opinion/2012/06/13/legal-profession-bill-2012-globalisation-strikes-lawyers/
    - http://www.malaysia.gov.my/EN/Main/MsianGov/GovConstitution/HistoryConstitution/Pages/HistoryofConstitution.aspx

7. Singapore[6]
    - http://www.singaporelaw.sg/content/LegalSyst1.html
    - http://www.legalservices.apec.org/inventory/singapore.html
    - http://www.lawsociety.org.sg/forMembers/ResourceCentre/RunningYourPractice/StartingaPractice/AGuidetoStartingaPractice/WhatEveryLawyerShouldKnow.aspx#14
    - http://www.lawsociety.org.sg/forMembers/ResourceCentre/RunningYourPractice/StartingaPractice/AGuidetoStartingaPractice/WhatEveryLawyerShouldKnow.aspx#7
    - http://statutes.agc.gov.sg/aol/search/display/view.w3p;page=0;query=CompId%3Aa320758b-b5c2-4c08-9ead-3ad55023b972%20ValidTime%3A20130124000000%20TransactionTime%3A20130124000000;rec=0

8. UK[7]
    - http://www.parliament.uk/about/
    - http://www.legalservicesboard.org.uk/
    - http://www.legaltutors.com/united_kingdom.htm
    - http://www.cabinetoffice.gov.uk/content/executive
    - http://www.historylearningsite.co.uk/the_judiciary.htm

---

[5] All the web sites accessed last on January 28, 2013.
[6] All the web sites accessed last on January 03, 2013.
[7] All the web sites accessed last on January 30, 2013.

- http://international.lawsociety.org.uk/ip/asia/1073/practise
- http://www.contactlaw.co.uk/court-structure-in-the-uk.html
- http://en.wikipedia.org/wiki/Law_of_the_United_Kingdom
- http://www.sra.org.uk/solicitors/handbook/code/content.page
- http://www.ucl.ac.uk/constitution-unit/research/uk-constitution
- http://london.stepbystep.com/ministry-of-justice-london-guide-19611/
- http://www.cilex.org.uk/about_cilex_lawyers/the_uk_legal_system.aspx
- http://www.ukti.gov.uk/investintheuk/whytheuk/lawandregulation.html
- http://www.college-of-law.co.uk/TwoColumn.aspx?id=5395&sctid=594
- http://ttallislaw.weebly.com/uploads/4/5/7/9/4579552/the_legal_system.pdf
- http://www.barcouncil.org.uk/becoming-a-barrister/how-to-become-a-barrister/
- http://www.lawgazette.co.uk/news/uk-legal-sector-set-benefit-hong-kong-investment
- http://www.royal.gov.uk/MonarchUK/QueenandGovernment/QueeninParliament.aspx
- http://www.ft.com/cms/s/0/723e2ffe-08b3-11e1-bc4d-00144feabdc0.html#axzz2JPnYsk1I
- http://www.royal.gov.uk/MonarchUK/QueenandGovernment/QueenandPrimeMinister.aspx
- http://www.lawsociety.org.uk/advice/practice-notes/setting-up-a-practice-regulatory-requirements/

9. USA[8]
    - http://www.americanbar.org/utility/about_the_aba.html
    - http://www.law.harvard.edu/programs/plp/pages/statistics.php
    - http://www.nycbar.org/small-law-firm-center/slf-resources/767-slf-faqs
    - http://www.laurencesimons.com/international-lawyers-admission-to-the-united-states
    - http://apps.americanbar.org/litigation/litigationnews/top_stories/professional-liability-insurance-states.html
    - http://www.americanbar.org/groups/professional_responsibility/publications/model_rules_of_professional_conduct/rule_7_2_advertising.html

---

[8] All the web sites accessed last on January 30, 2013.

Index*

advertising, regulations on, 56–58
Advocates Act, 1961, 71, 74–79, 87–89
All India Bar Examination (AIBE), 75, 79
alternative business structures (ABSs), 55
American Bar Association (ABA), 57, 58, 59, 63

Bar Council of India (BCI), 71, 74
Bar Professional Training Course (BPTC), 52
business process outsourcing (BPO), 24n5, 88

central product classification (CPC), 22–24
Companies Act, 1956, 69n2, 72, 73
Companies Act, 2013, 69n2, 72, 73, 103, 104, 149, 160
compound annual growth rate (CAGR), 26, 27, 28
conduct regulations, 65, 67, 68t, 179t
continuing legal education (CLE), 53, 111–113
continuing professional development (CPD), 49, 51, 52
cross-country indicators, 6t, 65 68, 66f, 67t

entry regulations, foreign legal professionals, 59–63

European Community (EC), 9
European Union (EU), 17, 18, 22, 26, 121n14, 135

Fly-in-fly-out, 88, 90, 121, 129, 130, 140, 141, 143, 152
Foreign Direct Investment (FDI), 64–65
Foreign Investment Promotion Board (FIPB), 87
foreign law firms (FLFs), 19, 60, 61
foreign legal consultant (FLC), 19, 21
formal law alliance (FLA), 54, 63
Free Trade Agreements (FTA), 90–91

Gaikokuho–Jimu–Bengoshi (GJB), 62
General Agreement on Tariffs and Trade (GATT), 20
General Agreement on Trade in Services (GATS), 1, 5, 6, 20–25
Globalization of legal services, 16, 18–22

High Court, 47, 71, 75
  Bombay, 87, 88, 116n12
  Madras, 88, 152

indemnity insurance requirements, 58–59
India, legal services in
  Advocates Act, 1961, 74–77
  Bar Council of India, 74
  BCI Rules, 1975, 77–79

* 't' signifies table, 'n' signifies note, and 'f' signifies figure.

domestic firms, 81–82
exports and imports, 85f, 85t
foreign firms, 82–84
foreign law firms, 86–89
Free Trade Agreements (FTAs), 90–91
GATS and revised offer, 89–90
historical evolution, 70–71
liberalizing legal services, 85–86
Limited Liability Partnership Act, 2008, 73–74
mutual recognition agreements, 91–92
Partnership Act, 1932, 72–73
regulatory environment, 79
regulatory framework, 71–72, 79–80
trade, 84
training and capacity building, 80–81
initial public offering (IPO), 134
Intellectual Property Rights (IPR), 25, 111, 138
international trade in legal services, 25

Japanese Federation of Bar Associations (JFBA), 49, 50, 62
Joint Economic and Trade Committee (JETCO), 124
joint law venture (JLV), 54, 63
Joint Ventures (JV), 62, 84, 94, 125, 137, 142
Juris Doctor (JD), 49, 52

law firms
 foreign law firms, FDI regulations for, 64–65
 foreign operations of, 30–31
 growth of, 28–29, 29f, 29t–30t
Law Society of England and Wales, 100
Legal Practice Course (LPC), 52
Legal Process Outsourcing (LPO), 107, 115, 129, 138, 152, 161

Legal Profession Act (LPA), 53
legal services liberalization. *See also* India, legal services in
 GATS, 20–25
 history of, 18–22
 NAFTA, 18–20
legal services restrictiveness indices
 OECD, 33–35, 34f
 World Bank restrictiveness indices, 35–37, 36f, 37t
Legal Services: Global Industry Guide (Datamonitor), 26
limited liability partnership (LLP), 53–55
Limited Liability Partnership Act, 2008, 72–74
LPA. *See* Legal Profession Act (LPA)
LPC. *See* Legal Practice Course (LPC)

market size
 Asia-Pacific, 26f
 Europe, 26f
 foreign operations of law firms, 30–31
 global legal services market segmentation, 27
 issues, trade in legal services, 31–32
 law firms, growth of, 28–29, 29f, 29t–30t
 US, 26f
multidisciplinary partnerships (MDPs), 43, 53, 103, 107, 108
multinational corporations (MNC), 123, 133, 135
mutual recognition agreements (MRA), 32, 91, 134, 135

New South Wales (NSW), 42
North American Free Trade Agreement (NAFTA), 1, 5, 18–19

Organization for Economic Co-operation and Development (OECD), 33–35, 34f

OECD Indicators of Product Market
  Regulation, 66f, 67t, 68t, 181t

Partnership Act, 1932, 73,74
political economy
  advertising restrictions, 99–102
  arguments, 146–149, 149–150
  business-related concerns, 123–127
  competitive disadvantages, 131–134
  convergence, 150–153
  disciplinary mechanisms, 118–119
  domestic market, benefits to,
    137–142
  employment-related concerns,
    127–129
  governance issues, 114
  governance-related concerns,
    129–131
  inconsistencies in views, 146–149
  issues and concerns, 119–120
  misperceptions, 143–145
  misplaced fears, 143–145
  preparedness and capacity, 111–114
  pros and cons, 121–123
  reciprocity, lack of, 134–137
  regulatory and challenges, 98–99
  regulatory barriers, 99
  regulatory framework, 114
  regulatory mandate, 117–118
  regulatory setup, 114–117
  representation issues, 114–117
  scale, 102–111
  scope, 118–119
  scope, and liability restrictions,
    102–111
  survey, 96–98
  uncertain benefits, 131–134
Postgraduate Law Course (PLC), 51
Practical Legal Training (PLT), 48, 49
preferential trade agreements (PTAs),
  91n14
professional services
  liberalization, 11–14
  regulation, 7–11

Professional Skills Course (PSC), 52
public–private partnership (PPP), 70,
  138
pupillage training organization (PTO),
  52

Qualified Foreign Law Firm (QFLF),
  61

reforms, roadmap for
  broad initiatives, 156–157
  capacity building measures,
    161–162
  regulatory structure, 157–158
  relaxing regulatory restrictions,
    160–161
  sector preparation, 159–160
  strengthening governance,
    158–159
  targeted measures, 157
  timeline for, 162–164
Regional Trade Agreement (RTA), 91
Registered European Lawyer (REL),
  52, 55
regulatory environment
  advertising serves, 40–41
  entry, restrictions, 39–40
  fees regulations, 41–42
  framework for legal services,
    38–44
  in selected countries, 44–50
  legal systems, 44–45
  organizational form, 42–44
  practice requirements, 48–53
  regulatory frameworks, 45–48

Self-regulation, 8–11, 15, 40, 114,
  117, 118
Services Trade Restrictiveness Index
  (STRI), 33, 34f, 35
Small and Medium Enterprises
  (SMEs), 13, 61
Solicitors Regulation Authority
  (SRA), 55, 57, 58

Supreme Court, 50, 71, 75, 76,
    87–89
Surrogate entry, 129

Trade in Services Agreement (TISA),
    121
trade, legal services
    GATS, 22–25
    history of liberalization, 18–22
    international trade, 25
    market size, 26–32

restrictiveness indices, 32–37
World Bank restrictiveness indices,
    35–37

United Nations Central Product
    Classification (UNCPC), 22

World Bank restrictiveness indices,
    35–37, 36f, 37t
World Trade Organization (WTO),
    1, 20, 22, 28, 35

About The Authors

Rupa Chanda is a Professor of economics and social sciences at the Indian Institute of Management, Bangalore. She has a PhD degree in Economics from Columbia University, with a specialization in International Trade, and a Bachelor's degree in Economics from Harvard University. She teaches macroeconomics and international trade and has received several teaching awards. Earlier, she has worked as an economist at the International Monetary Fund (IMF) in Washington, D.C. Professor Chanda's research interest's concern international trade in services, the World Trade Organization (WTO), and migration. She has been a member of the Ministry of Commerce's Expert Group on Services and the Planning Commission's High Level Group on Services, and is a member of various other government committees. She has undertaken research and consulting assignments for several multilateral and Indian organizations. Professor Chanda has many journal publications, chapters in books, and academic reports to her credit. Her books include: *Integrating Services in South Asia: Trade, Investment, and Mobility* (2011), *Globalization of Services: India's Opportunities and Constraints* (2002), and *India's Trade in Services: Prospects and Strategies* (2006). She has also presented her work in India and abroad.

Pralok Gupta is working as an Assistant Professor (Services and Investment) at the Centre for WTO Studies, Indian Institute of Foreign Trade, New Delhi. Dr Gupta has a PhD degree in Economics and Social Sciences from IIM Bangalore. He has been a visiting and full-time faculty member at various Indian institutions, including the Indo-German Chamber of Commerce. Dr Gupta has been appointed as member of the Task Force on Services Sector Exports, Ministry of

Commerce, Government of India; Member (Sectoral Expert) of the Inter Ministerial Sub-Group on Data in Trade in Services, Ministry of Commerce, Government of India; and member of the Technical Group on Data in Trade in Services under the chairmanship of the Director General of Commercial Intelligence and Statistics. He has been associated with various consultancy and research projects for corporate bodies, the government and international and multilateral institutions, such as the OECD, the British High Commission, UKIERI, European University Institute, South African Institute of International Affairs, etc. His research interests include economics of services trade, FDI in services, regulatory environment and trade policies, WTO and related Issues, trade and environment concerns, and international migration.